Praise for

101 Questions You Need to Ask in Your Twenties

Paul Angone has done it again! With his *signature sauce* of wit, warmth, and wisdom, he cuts right to the core of what's most essential with this book of crucial life lessons—and questions— for your twenties, thirties, and beyond. As Paul says in the book, "To find good answers, we must first ask good questions." Here are 101 to get you started. You'll be laughing, smiling, sighing with relief, and pondering—and beyond that, better able to adapt and change when faced with those unanswered prayers and plans that inevitably go awry, all for the sake of helping you grow into your best, biggest life.

Jenny Blake
Author of *Pivot: The Only Move That Matters Is Your Next One and Life After College*

Angone, who wrote the uber-popular *101 Secrets For Your Twenties*, comes full force again with his new book. With his usual blend of humor, warmth, and hard truths, Angone throws dozens of gut-check questions right in your face like a splash of ice-cold water you never knew you always needed. *101 Questions You Need to Ask in Your Twenties* is sure to be the new blueprint to help any young professional or college graduate find their true north.

Danny Rubin
Author of *Wait, How Do I Write This Email?: Game-Changing Templates for Networking and the Job Search*

As one who didn't start "getting it" until my 30s (better late than never, right?), I found myself wondering how much faster I'd have come to know (and genuinely dig) myself had a copy of this book showed up on my doorstep as I grappled with the life, relationship, and career decisions that rough most of us up throughout our 20s.

Jenny Foss
Career strategist and founder of JobJenny.com

Paul has a way of sharing his own story to make you laugh and let you know he's been there, but also encouraging you to look inside yourself to answer the tough questions to move your life forward. I can't think of a twentysomething who wouldn't benefit from having this smart book on their bookshelf.

Molly Beck
Author of *Reach Out* and founder of MessyBun.com

If you only read one book in your twenties, and I hope you read more, then make it this one. It's an essential list of questions we all need to be asking ourselves at every stage of life, especially young adulthood. Seriously. It's that good.

Jeff Goins
Bestselling author of *The Art of Work*

101

Questions

You Need to Ask

in Your

Twenties

(and let's be honest, your thirties too)

PAUL ANGONE

MOODY PUBLISHERS

CHICAGO

To my son, Judah.

May your life be full of

wisdom,

creativity,

and great friends

asking you good questions.

Edited by Connor Sterchi
Cover and interior design: Erik M. Peterson

Library of Congress Cataloging-in-Publication Data
Names: Angone, Paul, author.
Title: 101 questions you need to ask in your twenties : (and let's be honest,
   your thirties too) / Paul Angone.
Description: Chicago, IL : Moody Publishers, [2018]
Identifiers: LCCN 2018004060 (print) | LCCN 2018001216 (ebook) | ISBN
   9780802496539 (ebook) | ISBN 9780802416919
Subjects: LCSH: Young adults--United States. | Young adults--Life skills
   guides. | Conduct of life. | Success.
Classification: LCC HQ799.7 (print) | LCC HQ799.7 .A539 2018 (ebook) |
DDC
   305.2420973--dc23
LC record available at https://lccn.loc.gov/2018004060
ISBN: 978-0-8024-1691-9

We hope you enjoy this book from Moody Publishers. Our goal is to
provide high-quality, thought-provoking books and products that connect
truth to your real needs and challenges. For more information on other books
and products written and produced from a biblical perspective, go to
www.moodypublishers.com or write to:

Moody Publishers
820 N. LaSalle Boulevard
Chicago, IL 60610

3 5 7 9 10 8 6 4 2

Printed in the United States of America

Contents

Introduction:
Knocked Out Cold

There I was at the bottom of a 15-foot hill that I'd apparently just rolled down, lying face-first in weeds and shrubs, in a full baseball uniform, unconscious.

Definitely a unique place to find yourself on a Saturday afternoon.

Where am I? Did someone just hit me in the head with a baseball bat?

As I became conscious, these were the questions stumbling through my mind, like a surgery patient who'd just come to.

How in the world did I get here?

You see, fifteen minutes earlier I was sitting in the dugout with my college baseball team. I wasn't starting in the game, so I had a front-row seat to watch our weekly routine of getting absolutely crushed by the team we were playing.

To say we were a bad baseball team would be a polite way to put it.

Since we usually played two games every Saturday, and since the other team would score run after run after run after run to their sheer delight, this made for a very long, depressing day. Every Saturday, while all our friends were at the beach (because they certainly

9

didn't want to watch our game and subject themselves to that kind of misery), we just sat and stared at our own sadness for hours.

So when you were sitting the bench, like I was that Saturday with a handful of other teammates, it was a treat, a reprieve, a needed escape, to be the one to find a foul ball that was just hit.

Our baseball field stood above what we called the barrancas, a steep gully filled with dense, wild California plants, eucalyptus trees, and a small stream that cut through it. Trying to find a foul ball shot into this dense, wild greenery felt like being an explorer trying to locate the fabled city of gold—a grand adventure that was probably going to turn up empty-handed. But heck, when your other option was watching your team lose again by 20 runs, you searched for that ball with the diligence of Cortés!

On this fateful Saturday, as I saw the foul ball fly above our back-stop and into the barrancas, I shot out of the dugout, my mind and body ready to escape from our baseball cage. Plus, your best chance of actually finding the ball was to somehow spot where it landed or see it bounce off some rock and into the air. I quickly ran on a path under our wood bleachers on top of a ridge by the barrancas, my eyes looking out for the ball, when *bam*, everything went black.

Thus me, at the bottom of the barrancas, completely bewildered after being knocked out cold like a fish getting hit with an oar.

As the lights came on again in my mind, I stood up, fists clinched, ready to defend myself against my attacker. Yet, as I rose to my feet like a one-year-old trying to stand for the first time, no one was around. Above the hill, I could hear the sounds of a baseball game still being played, yet no one was in eyesight of me. So with pieces of leaves and weeds clinging to my uniform like POWs clinging to the rope of their rescue helicopter, I slowly started climbing back up the hill.

Discombobulated and hopelessly confused, all I could think of was one question: *what the heck just happened?*

THE STORY OF OUR TWENTIES AND THIRTIES

Our twenties and thirties can feel strangely similar, can't they? I know they did for me. Confused, discombobulated, wondering: *how the heck did I end up here?*

Before you reach your twenties you have all these big plans and dreams that you're so sure of. You nurtured these plans your entire life. Fed them. Loved them. Taught them how to read.

Then you leave college graduation, emerge into adulthood, and your plans run off with a biker gang in the middle of the night, and the last time you hear from them they're somewhere in Franklin, Kentucky, working at the Piggly Wiggly.

Growing up, we spend most of our lives climbing one stair after another. Middle school. High school. Get into the right college. Pick the best major. Get good grades. Land the right internship. Keep climbing those steps. Faster! Higher! Don't look back! Don't ask questions! *Just keep climbing!*

Because success is up there somewhere. You'll get to the top, fling open that door, and there will be your dream job, your dream house, dream spouse—basically an amazing, enviable, successful life where all your hard work climbing those steps will be clearly rewarded.

When I got to the top of the stairs after college graduation and swung open the door, I pictured walking into a place like Google. Where it's so cool it doesn't even feel like work. Where you're just drinking espresso, playing foosball, solving meaningful and significant problems, and laughing all day about nothing in particular, just because you're just so excited to work there.

Instead, I climbed all those steps. Got the good grades. Did the internships. And when I flung open that door and stepped inside, it looked a lot less like Google and more like a basement from a Stephen King made-for-TV movie.

As I made those first few steps into "my future" and was met with the unmistakable sound of the door quickly locking behind me, I started exploring the dark, dingy, barely lit halls filled with over-turned couches, broken-down Hondas, and Top Ramen wrappers. All I had with me was a resume, which I handed to a balding, mid-level manager sitting at a desk under a lone light bulb, only to have him take one look and laugh like I'd just told him some ridiculous joke.

I felt confused, afraid, and alone—those visions of making a difference while making a lot of money quickly changing into just making it through another day. In these dark halls, I'd occasionally bump into other twentysomethings, clearly as confused as me and muttering, *I wasn't supposed to end up here.*

REPEATING THE CLIMB

How did I end up here? It was the question I kept asking as I picked the grass and leaves off my jersey before clawing my way back up the barrancas after lying there unconscious. *How long was I out?* I didn't have a clue.

Okay, I was looking for a foul ball. This much I could remember.

So I went to the opposite side of the stands, where the opposing team's dugout and fans were, and began looking for the baseball again. In what must have looked like a drunken stupor, I stumbled around their fans, looking toward the ground, when someone finally asked me, "Um, excuse me, son, what are you doing? Are you okay?"

"Umm, yeah, uh, I'm looking for that foul ball that was hit over here," I said, trying to project some sort of confidence that I knew what I was doing.

The fan just stared at me for a moment with his head tilted like he was staring at one of those optical illusions, trying to see the real picture emerge.

"Um, so, the only ball that's come even close to here I found and threw back in. That was about fifteen minutes ago."

"Oh, yeah. Okay, sure," I said, turning back toward my dugout, more confused than ever.

"Hey, Paul, where have you been?" Cody, one my best friends on the team, sat down next to me at the end of the dugout bench, trying to be as quiet and discreet as possible as to not anger our head coach (who didn't exactly care for casual conversations in the dugout when we were losing by twenty runs). "Were you eating a hot dog out there or something? Why didn't you bring me one?" he asked, thinking I'd been having a grand old time at the concession stand without him.

"I think I just knocked myself out," I whispered, staring ahead.

"Ha! *What?*" Cody blurted out, eyes from our teammates shooting our way telling us to knock it off unless we all wanted to run sprints after the game. "What?" Cody whispered. "You knocked yourself out? What do you mean?"

"I have no idea. But I woke up, face first, at the bottom of the barrancas."

"*What!*" Cody let out again, this time receiving the cold, hard stare from our coach behind his sunglasses. "But you've been gone like twenty minutes," Cody said in as hushed a voice as his curiosity could muster.

"Yeah, so I've been told. I have no idea what happened."

After the game, word slowly spread that I'd somehow knocked myself out. How it all happened was still a complete mystery to me. A mystery that brought back a handful of teammates to the field afterwards, the last place we wanted to be after a 27–2 loss, to try and solve it.

But what did happen? We started retracing my steps and asking good questions to find the answer.

THE POWER AND IMPORTANCE OF GOOD QUESTIONS

To find good answers, we must first ask good questions. I believe there's nothing more powerful and important in our twenties than the questions we bring to it. Of course I do—I've written a whole book about it!

My friend Brent told me about a conversation he had with an extremely intelligent gentleman who specializes in artificial intelligence and automated bots. With the rise of automation and more sophisticated technologies, Brent asked this man what he felt his daughters needed to be good at to succeed as they grew up. The gentleman responded without missing a beat, "The ability to ask really good questions."

A good question is a problem half-solved, Brent loves saying. He's right. There's nothing more important when solving problems in our lives than the questions we are bringing to them.

As Dr. Meg Jay so aptly defined, our twenties are the "defining decade" of our lives. We are setting the course for our future. Yet, for years in my twenties I felt like my ship was sailing around in circles, colliding with every iceberg out there.

I think we all learn at some point that "groan up" life is not as easy as it looked on the front of the brochure. After college graduation and throughout our twenties, it can feel like we're experiencing a quarter-life crisis right after we got done with our last quarter-life crisis. And we're still not quite sure what a quarter-life crisis actually is, just the fact that we can't quite escape from having one.

Yet, there's one giant truth to being successful in our twenties. A simple fact that took me the whole decade to comprehend and appreciate:

Your twenties aren't about them going as you planned. But how you adapt, change, and grow when they don't.

Being successful in your twenties is about being purposeful in the process.

Your twenties will be covered in eraser marks and revisions. That's how it's supposed to be. Failure only happens if you stop writing. When you give up on the next page, leaving it blank when the heart of your story was about to unfold.

Asking the right questions. It's the only answer I've found. It's the only way to create a strategic framework to point your ship in the right direction before you start sailing. Then as well, good questions guide you along the journey as you constantly tack, pivot, and reconfigure as your journey goes further and deeper.

If you don't start with good questions, and keep asking yourself these questions as you are called to adapt and change, how can you formulate any worthwhile answers? If your journey starts with faulty premises and incomplete answers, then you'll end up traveling far off course, becoming stranded on some piece of land like Tom Hanks in *Cast Away*, yelling at a volleyball that also happens to be your closest friend. It doesn't make much sense.

And don't get me wrong, this process isn't always easy. It takes grit, honesty, and courage. Some questions are asked and left unanswered. For years. And that doesn't mean anything is wrong necessarily, it just means an answer may be yet to be determined. Some unanswered questions make you want to wear sweatpants all day and eat chocolate fried bacon. At work. For a month straight. It's a confusing time of life.

Yet, on the flipside, if we don't ask ourselves these questions, we can fall into the trap of a complacent life where we become comfortable with feeling miserable because we didn't want to ask ourselves any of the "hard" questions.

When we start believing the voice of the critics and cynics who try to convince us that it shouldn't matter that we want our work and life to matter—that's the scariest place to be. That's the path to slow death. Do not be sorry for not being apologetic that you want your life to mean something. I think we should live on purpose with purpose for a purpose. How about you?

CURING OUR OBSESSIVE COMPARISON DISORDER

As I first defined and discussed in *101 Secrets For Your Twenties*, as a generation we're struggling with an additional kind of OCD—Obsessive Comparison Disorder. And since I first coined, defined, and articulated this concept, people are constantly asking me what the best cure for Obsessive Comparison Disorder is.

Well, you're holding a great cure in your hands. As you go through these questions and struggle to find the best answers, you'll stop worrying so much about what other people are doing because you'll be focused on what *you* need to be doing. Obsessive Comparison Disorder has us constantly chasing other people's visions for their lives, while this book will help you create your own.

I believe each one of us has our own unique Signature Sauce—a mix of ingredients (strengths, talents, passions, experiences, etc.) that will taste like no one else's, giving the world a flavor and substance it desperately needs.

And asking ourselves these questions is the process toward discovering the recipe for your Signature Sauce. Just as a master chef explores and experiments until they've uncovered an amazing flavor just waiting to be discovered, you will uncover your purpose that's waiting to be revealed.

HOW TO READ THIS BOOK

For the last ten years, I've written books, studied, researched, and given my life to helping twentysomethings find the answers to truly living a successful and meaningful life. And the search for the right answers keeps bringing me back to finding the right questions.

I recommend trying to read this book through once without stopping too much to answer each question at first. Just get a feel for the book, the questions, stories, and insights woven together, before diving in and really trying to answer the questions in full. Maybe jot down a few notes, but keep going. Don't get stuck on a question and then not continue on through the whole book.

Then go through the book again and start really trying to wrestle with some of your answers, especially to the Signature Sauce questions. And if you start going through the questions and it becomes more difficult to find the answers than you thought it would be—*awesome*! That's normal. That means you're taking this seriously and being intentional.

Some questions are meant for you to tangibly answer on the page. Other questions are meant to just get you thinking. One question might take you two minutes to answer. Another question might take you two weeks.

I have tested these questions in live workshops with twentysomethings and with hundreds of people through my online course *Finding Your Signature Sauce*. I have written articles about them that have gone viral on the interwebs. I have tweaked, refined, and created a list of questions that I believe will help you get unstuck and help you move toward a more meaningful, significant life.

I've also included all the questions, organized within their sections, at the end of the book for you to cut out and put somewhere as a resource and reminder. Don't leave the questions alone in this book. Cut them out and take them with you.

Your situation and future story will change to the level you're willing to ask yourself these questions. And claw your way to answers, if need be. **I've definitely found over the years that oftentimes the hardest person to be honest with is myself.**

Yet, this is not a test. This is not a one-time thing. This is a lifelong process. Hopefully, this book can be a reference guide for the rest of your life. Something you can keep coming back to and tweak, change, and add to from this point on. Even when you're well beyond your twenties.

Grab a few friends and work through these questions together. **Community stokes clarity.**

SO, HOW DID I KNOCK MYSELF OUT?

As my teammates and I retraced my steps and asked ourselves pointed questions, we began finding the answers. We retraced my path that went under the wood bleachers, which appeared to all of us to have a high enough clearance that you couldn't hit your head on the wood overhang above.

Yet, there was one little spot where the ground went up a tad and if you stepped on it just right, it was the perfect height for the top of my head to slam into the wood overhang. When I was running, my eyes were down and to the left, looking for a ball, so when I took a step up in mid-jog in that exact spot, I completely blindsided myself with the large wood overhang that wasn't moving, and just rapidly introduced my head directly into it.

My teammates and I cut through my confused memory and solved the mystery by asking ourselves good questions. Sure, it wasn't the *least* embarrassing thing in the world to tell everyone at my college (and now in this book!) that I knocked myself out cold. But hey, at least I knew the answer to the mystery. And I had a good, embarrassing story to tell for the rest of my life. And I never made the same mistake again! Shoulder pat to me.

When you're not sure what happened. When you're trying to make sense of the nonsensical. When you're trying to clear the confused fog and find direction. When you're trying to figure out what *was*, so you can figure out what *should be*, there's only one answer—and that's asking yourself, and others, really good questions.

So wherever you find yourself right now. Whether at the top of the stairs, ready to fling open that door to your dream life. Or at the bottom like I was, confused and discombobulated, picking pieces of grass out of your hair as you wonder *how in the heck did*

I end up here? Let's start asking ourselves good, strategic questions.

Sure, clawing our way up the hill and to the answers might get a little difficult and messy at times. But I'd rather struggle to ask myself the right questions now than be plagued with one giant question when I'm old and gray: *what could have been?*

What's the best way to break up with myself?

Have you ever gone through a bad breakup?

I have.

I once drove a total of 18 hours in torrential rain to meet my girlfriend's parents, upon her request, where the parent meet-and-greet went amazing, and I left feeling like this could be "The One."

Then on the drive home, in the hurricane-esque rain, both sides of the highway I was trying to get home on were shut down—a mudslide wiping out one side of the highway and a semitruck turned over on the other, so I was ushered into a field with hundreds of other cars to wait for the highway to open up. I called my girlfriend to give her the update and her first response was—"Paul, we need to talk."

This wasn't "Paul we need to talk" about how amazing you are and our life together with our 2.4 kids.

No, she then proceeded to break up with me while I sat in my Honda, in a field, in the pouring rain, after driving 18 hours to meet her parents. I felt like I was living in a *Dawson's Creek* episode.

The next day after a breakup is surreal, isn't it?

When you wake up the next morning and don't know what to do with yourself. So at 9:00 a.m. you find yourself crumbling up Oreos into a peanut butter jar and eating it with a spork while you watch a TV marathon of *Gilmore Girls*. For three days straight. Your roommates pleading with you to do something, *anything*—for your health of course, but also because of the unmistakable "breakup odor" you're beginning to bless the entire house with.

Breakups are extremely tough because so much of your identity, plans, and future was wrapped up in that other person. When that is taken away, you feel lost.

Most life transitions are pretty similar to a bad breakup, aren't they?

But instead of breaking up with someone else, you're breaking up with a season of your life and who you were during that time. You're not only leaving a place behind, but you're also leaving behind a version of yourself. **In life transitions, you're kind of breaking up with yourself.**

And just like the time the relationship you were so sure about met its dramatic end, there's a real sense of wondering and wandering when you leave behind who you were.

Sure, there are mementos of you from the past that you'll carry with you. But the moment you leave who you were is the moment you begin the epic search to find out who you really are.

TRANSITIONS ARE HARD

Yet, we talk about life transitions like they're so simple. So light and breezy.

I'm just going through a bit of a transition.

No big deal, right?

Wrong.

Transitions can come like a punch in the gut when you're looking the other way.

Do you know what our introduction to the concept of transition was? Birth!

And while I thankfully don't remember mine, I have now experienced up close and personal the birth of my three children, and that's when I realized for the first time that it was possible to cry, throw up in your mouth, and pass out—all at the same time. And that's just as the husband who isn't exactly doing any of the actual work.

They even call the last phase of birth the "transitional" phase. And I think my wife would tell you, there's nothing light and breezy about it!

There's nothing simple about major life transitions and we're constantly going through them in life, especially during our twenties. Whether the transition is glaring—like college graduation, marriage, starting a new job, or unceremoniously getting laid off from the job you have—or the transition is discreet and gradual like the sun moving across the sky, slowly changing your perspective of the landscape around you, life transitions are a huge deal. They are most often the toughest seasons of life to go through while also being the most important.

There's something of strange significance that happens to us when we're stripped of everything we used to depend on.

Nothing feels comfortable when in transition. Nothing feels normal. In transitions, feeling completely abnormal becomes the new normal.

THE BIGGEST MISTAKE WE MAKE IN TRANSITION

Yet, here's the biggest mistake I think we make when going through transitions—we try to fly through them as fast as possible to get to the other side. We try to find and cling to some new normal. Yet, oftentimes in our desperation for permanence, we stop ourselves short instead of letting the transition help carry us to the destination we needed to get to.

Life in your twenties can especially feel like one perpetual transition. You have no idea where you're going, yet you're sure you can't stay here.

So right now if you feel like your life is in major transition, that's normal. Stay calm, hold on, and stay intentional.

Maybe transitions aren't something to fly through but something to marinate in.

Don't just make it through a transition—make the transition matter.

Transitions are not simply a bridge to the next important season of your life. Transitions *are* the most important seasons of your life.

As you walk through transition, what guides your way? Is it fear? Or is it faith?

Faith says, *This transition is taking me to a much better place. Keep moving forward.*

Fear says, *Take me back to what was. Even though it was terrible, at least I knew what to expect.*

Where is your transition trying to lead you? What is it telling you about the future you want to transition into? Take a moment and think about this.

Yes, transitions can feel like a bad breakup. But wouldn't you rather break up than stay in a dead-end relationship?

Am I struggling to make it appear like I'm not struggling?

We're all struggling. Yet, we're all struggling to make it look like we're not struggling.

The walls we build to protect our image only keep people away. We try to keep our wounded pride intact, while it's lying lifeless on the floor.

I've said it before, and I'll say it again right now because I know I need the reminder:

We don't connect with each other through our pretend perfection. We connect over our shared struggle.

Authenticity starts with you.

Be brave enough to go first.

What kind of friendships do I have—Jetpack Friends, helping me fly, or Anvil Friends, repeatedly pulling me down into some dark basement?

Your life will resemble the lives of your closest friends. Does that fact excite you or freak you out?

Are your friends taking purposeful steps forward in life or are they still playing beer-pong in the basement?

Do you leave after hanging out with friends feeling anxious or alive? Are your friends anvils tied around your ankles or jetpacks helping you fly?

Our friendships are never going to be perfect. And sometimes we have to help carry our friends through hard times, as they in turn will help carry us through ours. "Friending" in our twenties is bound to be awkward at times and hit many different rough patches. As I wrote in *101 Secrets For Your Twenties*, "Making and keeping friendships in your 20s is harder than G.I. Joe's abs." We have to be willing to take risks in our relationships. Pursuing some friendships through the awkward phases and then letting go of other friendships that continually take us down.

This is what I mean by an Anvil Friend, someone who continually is a bad influence or negative voice in your life. Someone who doesn't really want to see you change, grow, and be successful because they want you to stay stuck with them. If a "friend" does consistently more harm to you than any enemy would, I'm not sure this is the best kind of friend to hitch your life to.

So do you have more Anvil Friends, Jetpack Friends, or a mix of in-betweens? Well, let's figure this out.

List the five people below who you spend the most time with. Put a number between 1and 10 next to their name with a 1 being an Anvil Friend pulling you down and a 10 being a Jetpack Friend helping you fly. Then add up all the numbers to see what Friending Category you fit into below.

1.

2.

3.

4.

5.

FRIENDING SCORECARD

40-50: Your friends are going places, and they're taking you with them. Hold on for the ride!

30-39: You have some gems in there, but there might be one lump of coal pulling down your Christmas stocking.

20-29: Time to seriously start rethinking some of these "friendships." A bad friend is worse than a good enemy.

10-19: With friends like these who needs enemies?

1-9: Maybe it's time to move to Wyoming? Cows are pretty friendly.

If I'm going to pursue a big dream, am I willing to drive a 1993 Honda Civic Hatchback with no power steering, no air conditioning, and no right mirror for 15 years?

Pursuing something bigger than yourself will cost you something. So if you're going to pursue your purpose, what are you willing to sacrifice?

Thus, why I posed this question in Honda Civic Hatchback terms.

When I was 17-years-old, my dad was a pastor of a church, and a family who attended the church gave me a 1993 Honda Civic Hatchback. Being a pastor's kid has its drawbacks, sure—always sitting in the front row, while everyone judges every cough and time you start snoring. Oh, and that walk of shame when you show up ten minutes late and have to walk the long, green mile down the center aisle, everyone feeling more secure in their own salvation because at least they can show up to church on time. Unlike the pastor's family.

Then every mistake you make in high school is primed and ready to be choice church gossip to everyone's delight. It was like living in a reality show, without the fame or money!

But there were definitely perks of being a pastor's kid as well (mainly the fact that everyone knows your family doesn't have any money). And they want to snag some free points with God by helping your family out. And God bless them for it.

I was driving a 1977 Bonneville at the time that got seven miles to the gallon, while also having a gas gauge that didn't work (a fun realization during rush hour on day seven driving the car), so this Honda was a huge step up. I went from driving "The Tank" to driving "The Egg," and at pretty much every stage of my life, I've been made fun of for driving this car.

I bring this up because I'm still rolling around in The Egg to this day. And let me just admit that I'm just *a few* years north of high school graduation. And that Honda is currently running north of 240,000 miles!

I'm not opposed to having a nice car or a house someday. I've just been at peace sacrificing in those areas because other non-negotiables in my life were more important.

Then I just tell my kids that everyone who owns a big house is evil. So problem solved there. Kidding, of course. No, I just make my kids eat broccoli wrapped in kale every time they mention living in a big house. Then, when I mention living in an RV as a possible life idea for the family, and they get excited, I give them chicken nuggets and let them drink from the bottle of ketchup. Childhood conditioning done right.

Plus, my Honda Civic runs so low to the ground and starts shaking when it goes over 70 mph, so it feels like you're going dangerously fast at all times. Which my kids love.

The car was built without power steering, air conditioning, and no right mirror. Thank you Japanese efficiency. Even calling it a car is a bit of an overstatement. Oh, and the radio volume turns up on its own, which is always a fun surprise. It goes from "Classical Piano" volume to "Heavy Metal Screaming Directly in your Ear" in 2.3 seconds. Really it's the only thing the car does quickly.

But the car is so old and basic, it's cool. I'm a hipster in my kids' eyes, and they don't even know what a hipster is. I'm going to run with this as long as I can.

So in your career, your relationships, your life—what's going to be your Honda Civic Hatchback? Functional, yet not exactly something you're pulling up to valet parking.

What are you willing to give up, and what are you going to cling tight to?

Are you willing to move anywhere, but you don't want to take a job that expects more than 40 hours a week? Is job flexibility a nonnegotiable or is it job stability?

Do you need to create? Or lead? Work at a job that has a social impact? Or work at a job with a clear progression for financial gains?

Figuring out what you won't give up and what you will sacrifice will tell you a lot about what you should pursue.

Someday I won't be driving a 1993 Honda Civic Hatchback. Someday I'll be riding around in 2003 Honda with the resplendent air of a Saudi Arabian prince. But today's just not that day. Unless you tell about 30,000 friends to buy this book. Then, look out!

Write a list of three things you're willing to sacrifice to pursue something bigger in your life.

1.

2.

3.

Are there dark days ahead?

This question came out of a not-so-ordinary graduation speech by a not-so-ordinary speaker.

First, the speech was only four minutes long! A miracle in itself.

Second, and most importantly, the speaker that day wasn't just addressing the graduating class at Harrow School, but a whole country. And doing it with more power and truth in four minutes than most speakers deliver in a lifetime.

The graduation speaker? Winston Churchill. The year? 1941, as England stared down their complete annihilation in the hands of the Nazi army.

Yet, in the face of this harsh reality, Churchill spoke these words:

"Do not let us speak of darker days: let us speak rather of sterner days. These are not dark days; these are great days—the greatest days our country has ever lived; and we must all thank God that we have been allowed, each of us according to our stations, to play a part in making these days memorable in the history of our race."

Churchill knew dark days. Through his lifetime the battle with depression that he called his "black dog," to his political defeat that sent him in near political exile for the ten years leading up to the war, to only face Hitler and the near destruction of England.

Winston Churchill knew how dark darkness could get.

Yet, he made a call for a collective change of perspective. To not see the days ahead as dark, but as a great opportunity for great people to do great things for a great cause.

Churchill spoke to their collective purpose in the struggle instead of focusing on the pain.

And the even more amazing thing beyond these words that Churchill spoke was the loneliness, heavy unknowns, terror, and despair that he spoke these words into. France had just fallen to the Nazi army, England looked just months away from sharing the same fate, and the United States had not even entered the war yet.

Churchill was not speaking these words retroactively, looking back at the course of events that led them to victory. Churchill spoke these words in the face of utter destruction, yet he foresaw a radically different outcome than what the current facts at hand were shouting. He spoke into the face of destruction with hope and purpose. Then, he worked with all his heart to create that reality.

When we think about the tough times of our twenties, and there will be many. And the tough times we go through in the years after our twenties, and there will be many. Let us take to heart Churchill's cry to a generation embroiled in the toughest, yet greatest, days imaginable:

"Never give in. Never give in. Never, never, never, never—in nothing, great or small, large or petty—never give in, except to convictions of honor and good sense. Never yield to force. Never yield to the apparently overwhelming might of the enemy."

Do I love from my insecurities or from my strengths?

What's the difference?

Loving from your insecurities demands from others. Loving from your strengths gives to them.

Loving from your insecurities does not want to see people succeed more than yourself. Loving from your strengths hears of others' success and is the first to celebrate with them.

Loving from insecurities daily demands, "what are you going to do for me?" Loving from your strengths asks others, **"What can I do for you?"**

This is a question to ask in your friendships, dating relationships, marriage, etc.

If you "love" from your insecurities, your love will be needy and selfish. Loving from our insecurities can be the worst form of manipulation there is.

When someone loves from their strengths, they know who they are and are drawing from a deep, full well to give to you without demanding a drink in return.

I'm sure right now you can think of different people in your life and pinpoint who loves more from their strengths than their insecurities. There's a felt difference. A freedom in that relationship that encourages you to be the best version of yourself.

Too many people love from their insecurities, and that's not love.

Am I seeing the other side of people's Instagram photos (you know, the side they're not exactly posting pictures of)?

It was 5:30 a.m. as my wife and I were driving through the sunrise of the Arizona desert, as we tried to take as much ground before our three kids arose from their backseat slumber. Pinks and yellows shot across the sky and began to light up the red cliffs and mesas lining the highways as the white outline of the full moon paid its respects to the morning before it bid its farewell. It was one of those picturesque moments that you know a picture would never fully capture.

Staring up at this morning desert sky is when my wife, Naomi, made this point that struck me like a rock shooting up and hitting our windshield.

"You know, when we see people's success, it's like looking at the moon—you just see the side that's all lit up, but you don't see their dark side of the moon."

Her insight struck me as profound, even when running on only a few hours of sleep and gas station coffee on a 20-hour road-trip with three kids. So I knew there must be something to it!

I thought more about what she said. Even in their full glow, everyone has their dark side of the moon. No matter how successful they look, everyone has a side to their "groan up" life that is not exactly radiant or obvious to others.

Adulting is hard. As I wrote in my book *All Groan Up*, "You grow into growing up, each season bringing with it things you're going to have to secretly Google to figure out how to do." There's another side to everyone's Instagram photo that they're not exactly taking a picture of.

Take for example the picture I posted on Instagram of my family standing in front of Hanging Lake in the Colorado Rockies. It's a beautiful shot of my family huddled together in front of a majestic waterfall spilling into a clear, green lake thousands of feet up in the mountains. It was an unforgettable hike.

Yet, the reason we're all huddled together is because it snowed most of the hike! The reason it was so unforgettable was because at different points of the trip I seriously wondered if we were going to make it back alive. I started imagining us as the lead story on the ten o'clock news of the parents who stupidly took their kids on a hike, where at the bottom of the hike read big signs that basically said, "Hey, idiots! This hike is hard. Don't take young kids or dogs. We're not bringing the helicopter out to rescue you!"

At one point I was holding my eight-month-old in my arms, who was getting sicker by the moment, while carrying my four-year-old, who was crying uncontrollably, on my back. Actually, every kid was crying uncontrollably. Then of course, it started snowing extremely hard on the hike back down, a trail covered in slick, wet rocks. I slipped once and almost fell hard with two kids following me down to the rocks below.

Somehow we made it back down, but now whenever we mention going hiking, my kids start slightly twitching and begin faking injuries. Yet, you don't quite get this full story when you look at the picture I posted on Instagram.

There's always two sides to people's pictures, people's lives, people's stories, just like there's two sides of the moon. The sun cannot shine on all sides of the moon at once just as few people can honestly say that every aspect of their adult life feels significant or is working out like they planned. And those who do say that the loudest and proudest, I've learned the hard way, are usually the ones with the darkest sides of the moon in the sky.

As my wife continued her Road Trip Dark Side of the Moon Comparison Theory, another thought struck me about the moon.

Whether it looks like a sliver, barely visible in the sky behind clouds or it's giant and alive, no matter how the moon looks on a given night, the moon is always the same size.

For some people, their glow feels larger than life while other times our own glimmer feels like it's barely existent. Yet, we are all human. We are all the same size.

Significance and worth are not more or less available for anyone.

Even if it feels like someone else's significance is an overwhelming beam of light that hurts your eyes to look at, they are the same size as everyone else. You just can't see it from where you stand.

8

How do I get lost on purpose with purpose for a purpose (and not end up in some ravine, naked and eating bugs, wishing I would've just stayed indoors where it was safe)?

I feel lost.

I hear this phrase a lot. With all the ambiguity that comes from emerging into adulthood, who can blame us for feeling directionless?

Yet, when someone tells me they feel lost, I tell them, "That's amazing. I'm so glad you feel lost!"

And no I'm not being *that* guy who's rubbing their *lostness* in their face with my enviable sports car and $100,000 salary. Neither of which I have, of course. Unless by the time you're reading this book '93 Honda Civics have become so un-cool that they are now cool. And if that's the case, then *ha*, take that everyone who called my car The Egg!

No, it's really important to get lost. I know that now. Because you can't explore if you first don't know exactly where you are going.

ALL EXPLORERS HAVE TO FIRST GET LOST

I think as a generation we want to find our purpose.

We want to do something that means something.

Yet, we subconsciously expect the path to our purpose to be straightforward. We want to walk down a well-lit path with a cascading waterfall clearly in view from the start. At least, that was me in my early twenties.

If we can't handle ambiguity in life, we won't do anything great.

We have to get lost if we want to discover something new and amazing.

Sure, it might feel like you're going through a quarter-life crisis.

But maybe feeling lost is a healthy, important part of going through a transition.

Exploring and being lost are pretty much the same thing. The biggest difference is that explorers get lost on purpose with purpose for a purpose.

Explorers have a general sense of where they're going. They have guides to help them along the way.

They're not out there all alone.

Yet, the exact destination and how they're going to get there is completely unknown.

Explorers don't follow a map, they make the map as they go.

MIND-EXPLODING LOSTNESS

For many of us, this concept of being at peace while feeling lost is a complete mind-explosion. It definitely was for me in my twenties.

Because we grow up with clear, concise instructions on how to be successful.

We're given the syllabus at the start of class.

We have a college counselor lay out the next four years for us to graduate with honors.

Yet, "groan up" life is messy, full of zigzags, start-overs, and *what were you thinking?*

The path to your purpose is rarely straightforward.

The only way you'll find a clear direction is by first allowing yourself to get lost. In the next question, let's breakdown what some of those benefits might be.

YOUR TWENTIES AREN'T ABOUT THEM GOING AS YOU PLANNED. BUT HOW YOU ADAPT, CHANGE, AND GROW WHEN THEY DON'T.

PAUL ANGONE | *101 QUESTIONS YOU NEED TO ASK IN YOUR TWENTIES* | #101Q

9

Are there actually benefits to feeling lost?

> **"BEING LOST MIGHT BE THE EXACT SPOT THAT YOU WILL BE FOUND."**
> — *101 Secrets For Your Twenties*

Here are the six important things that happen to us when we feel lost:

1. When you're off-trail, your creativity is put to the test.

When you have to blaze the trail, you have to get creative. **Your genius is stoked when you're forced to actually use it.**

2. There's a bit of healthy danger that makes your senses come alive.

When you're off-trail, your senses are functioning at a higher level.

You're hearing more.

Seeing more.

Smelling, tasting, and touching in a way you can't, and won't, do when you're on a familiar path.

You take more in because you have to.

3. You're more capable of experiencing life's unexpected surprises.

You can't be surprised if you see everything clearly laid out in front of you.

4. You don't get the right answers. You get the right questions.

Succeeding in "groan up" life is not about always finding the right answers. It's about asking the right questions. And when you're lost in your twenties, the answers are incomplete.

When you're lost, you're ready to ask good questions because your life depends on it.

5. As you explore new territory, you find new parts of yourself.

Character is rarely developed sitting at a luxury resort.

Your character is being built when everything around you feels like it's crumbling.

Humility. Perseverance. Faith. Insight. Context. These aren't refined and defined when everything in your twenties makes complete sense.

When you don't know where you're going, you understand more about where you came from. **Ambiguity in life stokes clarity in character.**

6. Purpose is found in the struggle.

Your purpose is rarely honed in the clear-cut.

We don't find our purpose in spite of the struggle, we find it smack dab in the middle of it.

Do you feel lost? Congrats. You're officially exploring.

Take one step. Then another. You can't see what's up around the bend until you get there. When it feels like you want to turn back, remember—**the most exciting part of any journey is when you go off-trail.**

Should I really post this?

We've all been there. Where you've written your scathing report or sarcastic comment. Or you've uploaded that somewhat questionable photo. Now your finger is hovering over the "Post" button, and something stops you.

Should I really post this?

If you're asking the question, you probably already know the answer. Follow that instinct that's telling you to take your finger off the trigger.

You're creating your brand online with every single thing you share.

Once that shot is fired, there's no taking it back.

Job interviews are hard enough without them having your "dancing at the club" photos from spring break looking up at them from your job application folder.

When they ask you what you like to do for fun and you start telling them you like to feed homeless cats at the local church in your free time, I'm not sure they'll buy it.

11 ◆

Everything you think you know about marriage flies out the window once you're actually married. So what's the best way to know if you're actually ready to get married?

I was meeting with a longtime mentor of mine, and I asked him a question I'd been wrestling with for years—

"How do you know if you're ready to get married?"

His answer—

"You don't know you're ready to get married until you're actually married."

Well, that doesn't help much.

Sure, he was right. Sort of.

Everything you think you know about marriage flies out the window once you're actually married.

Yet, now that I'm married, I do believe there are some signs you're ready to get married. Or at least more ready than not.

So if you're dating or just freaked out about the idea of marriage in general. Or you've been married for years and can relate, read these five signs you're ready to get married.

5 SIGNS YOU'RE READY TO GET MARRIED

1. Right when your favorite song comes on, someone changes the radio station. And you don't freak out!

That moment in some shape or form, happens about once a week in marriage. If you can take some deep breaths and sometimes let your song, your plans, your ideas go, you might be ready for marriage.

If you have to fight to have "your song" on all the time in marriage, you're going to be fighting a lot.

2. The one thing you absolutely know is how much you don't. And you can live and breathe in that space.

Marriage has a funny way of challenging everything you were absolutely sure you knew. If you need to be right all the time, then in marriage you'll be absolutely wrong no matter how right you are (I might be speaking from stupid/stubborn experience here).

If you're as flexible as a piece of wood, then marriage will smack you upside the head with it.

3. You can clean a toilet.

And mop floors. Buy groceries. Pay bills. Basically you're becoming, you know, all "groan up" and stuff.

47

4. You're ready for a crazy adventure through the absolute depths and heights that life has to offer.

Picture the worst moment of your life.

Now picture the best.

Now picture someone standing right there next to you, holding your hand, trying to read your face through them both.

In marriage, you don't visit someone at their worst moment. No, you live with them through it.

If that doesn't freak you out too much, well saddle up partner, to holy matrimony.

But the real beauty of it—you learn more about how to love someone and what love is, *not* during the shareable social-media moments, but during those hard moments you don't want anyone else to see.

Honestly, having someone to share my life with, the good and the bad, is one of my favorite parts of marriage. It makes the bad a lot easier to get through and makes the good that much sweeter.

5. You're sick of sowing all those wild oats.

If you're throwing your oats out there like birdseed to pigeons, marriage might not be in the five-year plan.

If you're sick of sharing your oats with everyone only to get a bunch of pain and regret in return, and you'd rather have a nice, hot bowl of gluten-free oats at home, then marriage might be around the corner.

♦ 12

One of the best
ways to forget your
problems is by
helping someone
else with theirs, and
one of the best ways
to find perspective
is by looking
outside yourself.
So ask yourself—*who
can I help today*?
There's no lack of
"Help Wanted" signs.

13 ◆

Have I told anyone where I'm going?

Have you ever seen the movie *127 Hours*? It's an intense movie. A tough watch. And contains one of the most poignant messages and warnings for all of us that we need to take to heart.

If you haven't seen the movie, it stars James Franco, who does an incredible job portraying real-life mountain climber Aron Ralston and his harrowing account of falling down a canyon in remote Utah only to have a boulder land on his arm, preventing any escape.

Ralston is stuck. And as the intensity and enormity of the situation begins to set in, he realizes a cold, hard truth: *I never told anyone where I was going.*

No one would know where to look. No one would be coming to his rescue. **He was utterly alone because he lived his life like he never needed anyone.**

We don't need to be mountain climbers like Aron Ralston to heed this warning. There is a danger in going at anything completely alone. We need to tell people where we are going and where we have been. And the remedy is something simple, yet extremely difficult: vulnerability.

ME BEING VULNERABLE

It's been over five years now since I left my "real job" to pursue being a full-time writer, speaker, coach, consultant.

And can I confess something to you?

Some months, I don't have a clue what the best next step is. Or where the money is going to come from next.

Obsessive Comparison Disorder seeps into my mind and heart as I look upon the lives of friends and wonder if I've royally screwed up mine. **Anxiety starts cascading through my body like a rogue helium machine filling me until I explode.**

I take a lot of walks, searching for clarity while simultaneously trying to escape that "*Am I completely blowing it?*" feeling. Fear slithers its fingers inside my chest and my heart feels *boa-constrictored*. My mind tells me one thing, my emotions another, and my legs tell me to run as fast as I can.

Why am I telling you all this?

If I sing about the need for all of us to be authentic and vulnerable, while I inauthentically hide behind each piece of advice and the exciting parts of my journey, then I'm just another clanging symbol amidst a cacophony of unnecessary noise.

We all need people in our lives to tell where we are going. I've talked a lot about being lost and exploring, yet we shouldn't be going on this journey alone.

It takes a lot of courage to talk about where you lack the most courage. We have to be courageous enough to open the doors and let others really see inside. We all need to be brave enough to be vulnerable.

And honestly, if I can just get *really* real with you right now. I wouldn't be able to handle any of this if I didn't truly believe and know that God is here with me in all my questions, imperfections, insecurities, and fears. If I didn't sense in my spirit Him saying, "Relax. We're in this together," I would be an inoperable mess.

I can't do surgery on myself. Or at least, I don't want to try.

So here's a piece of my struggle for you to see inside. To hopefully encourage you in yours. Whether you feel like you're failing, you're smack dab in the middle of a quarter-life crisis, losing inspiration, or you just can't seem to feel normal again.

"Groan up" life is hard and we can't do it alone. Let's keep exploring, yet ask people to walk with us along the way.

We're not supposed to ease the angst by pretending like it's not there. There are answers in the angst if we're willing to vulnerably sit in it and ask the hard questions.

I don't have it all figured out, but I know I'm not supposed to.

Explore. Get lost.

But tell people where you are and where you are going. So that if the rock falls on your arm, you'll have someone there to help you get it off.

How do I make a choice when I don't know what to choose?

Today more than ever, we are suffocating in choices. Options. Possibilities. What ifs. A Google search supplying you with three million results and counting.

Every choice you make means you're *not* choosing a million other options.

Whether it's choosing the right place to live, the right spouse, the right career, the right Spotify station, the right Pad Thai, or what the heck to watch on Netflix, every decision feels like an anxiety attack waiting to pounce, claws first.

How do you deal with all these choices in your twenties? And even better, how do we find some way to make the right choices without driving ourselves crazy?

First, when you don't know what to choose, make a choice that you're going to choose something.

It sounds straightforward. But we become so paralyzed in choosing something that we end up choosing nothing instead.

Not making a choice is a choice. And probably the least constructive choice you can make.

Because you don't learn anything staying in the same place. Just like a river, when water stops going downstream, it becomes a place where muck, mire, and sickness set in.

We need to keep flowing downstream even if we don't know exactly what awaits us around the bend.

As Teddy Roosevelt so aptly put it:

"Get action. Do things; be sane; don't fritter away your time; create, act, take a place wherever you are and be somebody; get action."

Make a choice that you're going to make a choice. Find your "I'm 77% sure" and give it a try. You won't know how it's all going to work out until you start doing the work.

If you're struggling to figure out what your passion is and what you want to pursue, pick something. Answer some of the questions in this book, make as strategic of a choice you can, then move forward.

If it doesn't work out, that's great. Well, maybe not exactly great. But every time you figure out what you don't want to do, you come one step closer to figuring out what you *do* want.

It's a game of emerging adult elimination. Every time you cross something off the list, you get closer to naming a winner.

Climbing through your twenties can feel like being a pug trying to scale a mountain. It's loud, ungraceful, and feels like all eyes are on your slow climb.

But one tiny step after another, and you'll make it to the view you forgot you were climbing for. To everyone's disbelief. I promise.

Get action. Don't wait.

Drowning in options is a terrible way to die.

Do it big. Do it small. Just do something.

15

ADULT

What is fear keeping me from doing? Is it worth it?

I still remember crawling through a tent-tunnel with my two-year-old daughter when my phone notified me I had an email. An email that I stood up in sheer excitement after reading, forgetting I was in a tent-tunnel, that was now hanging off me in pieces while my daughter stared at daddy apparently officially losing it.

The email was a reply to an email I almost didn't send. I talked myself out of sending this email for weeks. I was petrified to press send.

Yet, here I was reading a reply from a huge influencer in my life, whose books I've pored through, whom I've never met, and yet, here was Seth Godin endorsing my first book, *101 Secrets For Your Twenties*. I called to my wife in the kitchen with giddy excitement, holding the phone triumphantly in the air, tunnel dangling off my backsides.

If you don't know Seth Godin, you need to. The man breathes insight, wisdom, and inspiration in his amazing books and is a guru of business, marketing, influence, education, and leadership.

So with this current book years later, I thought of emailing Seth again, this time asking him what question he thought every twenty-something needs to ask themselves.

Again, I was scared to send the email. Again, I talked myself out of sending it for weeks. Again, I let fear get the best of me in the name of *"I don't want to waste Seth's time…"*

But then, I stopped stopping myself. I finally sent the email, breathed a sense of relief, and then started kicking myself for bothering him with a bothersome ask.

Then again he responded, with his question for every twentysomething:

"What is fear keeping you from doing? Is it worth it?"

It's like Seth read through the fear and trembling pouring through the fingers that had written him.

Fear had stopped me many times. Yet, Seth was right, of course. It wasn't worth it.

What is fear holding you back from? Is it worth it? Is it worth the anxiety that comes from letting fear get the best of you? Is it worth never knowing? Is it worth living a life of "if onlys"? Is it worth staying stagnant, comfortable yet miserable?

Never taking needed risks because of fear is not worth it. It typically never is. Trying and knowing is better than wondering *what if*.

Stop stopping yourself.

16

What would my life look like if I were okay just being me?

Have you ever been on a trail ride before?

Where you jump on a horse, adrenaline pumping, expecting to have the thrill ride of your life. And instead, you spend an hour slowly walking in circles around some trees on a horse with one foot in the grave. Instead of an epic adventure, you spend the whole time staring at the horse's posterior directly in front of you as your horse tries to get you as uncomfortably close to it as possible.

When I worked as a wrangler at a ranch in the Rocky Mountains where people would come to vacation, I took thousands of rides just like this. I personally didn't want anything "adventurous" to happen on these rides because that just meant a teenage girl's hair somehow got braided around a tree branch (horses love this game). Or a really scary little bunny jumped out from behind a bush and sent someone's horse running like that tiny bunny pulled a machine gun on it.

I tried many times to explain to the horses that they were just *slightly* larger than a cute little bunny. And that plastic bags blowing in the wind were not sent from the devil himself as agents of horse-terror. But apparently those huge horse ears are hard of hearing.

Yet, there were times when us wranglers would say goodbye to all the guests and take some horses out on our own kind of ride. The ride consisted of taking out horses that were not exactly "guest ready," as part of our job was breaking in horses that were a little on the crazy side.

On these rides, we'd take a few looks at each other, squeeze our horses with our heels, and the adventure would begin! We'd fly around trees as we foolishly played games like tag on horseback. Not something I'm recommending you do, nor something I'd do now, but it sure was fun at the time!

On one ride in particular with my friends Scott and John, we really worked our horses into a sweaty frenzy as we sprinted our way to the top of a ridge. I was riding my favorite horse on the ranch, a headstrong, fast, brown Quarter Horse named Hondo.

As we let the horses take a breather and looked down on the other side of the ridge to a fairly substantial decline, Scott said "Okay, I think we should take it a little easy and let our horses cool down. This is getting a little dangerous."

These words of wisdom from Scott, of course, cued John and me to take a glance at each other and go flying down the ridge side by side. And of course, we should have heeded Scott's warning.

As John and I flew on our horses, his horse decided he'd had enough of mine and head-butted my horse in the hip. My horse then proceeded to take off in another gear that I didn't know a horse had while John's horse shot the other way. I'd later find out that John then proceeded to hit his shoulder on a tree trunk, spin off his horse, and land in a bush. (He was okay, mostly!)

But I didn't know any of that was happening because Hondo was running full gallop down the middle of a valley as I attempted to slow him down.

Trees on the left and right of me whizzed past like still lifes turned blurred impressionism. Up ahead 50 yards I began to make out a large ravine coming our way.

Now, in my memory this "ravine" was Grand Canyon–esque. In actuality it was probably more a small, dry, creek bed, but as Hondo charged toward it with no intention of stopping, I knew that we were either going over or dangerously falling into it. Hondo did not miss a beat as he leapt over the ravine, and as I let out an warrior-like adrenaline shout, which I want to say sounded like John Wayne yelling at a wolf. When in actuality it probably sounded like a six-year-old girl who had a spider land on her arm.

We landed on the other side of this Grand Canyon–esque ravine that Evel Knievel would've surely been proud of as both Hondo and I stayed upright. Yet, as I got my wits and eyes looking forward again I saw a new obstacle up ahead—a wall of trees! I started pulling back hard, hoping that Hondo didn't have suicide on his mind today as he seemingly was not going to stop.

Fifty yards to the trees . . . 25 yards . . . *he's not going to stop* . . . pulling back with *all* I had . . . 10 yards . . . then bam, he put on the brakes. I lurched forward, found myself more on the horse's neck than on his back, but we were stopped. And we were alive!

My heart pounding in my chest as I could feel Hondo's pounding in his, I sat back on the saddle and my first reaction was to praise God.

One, because I was still alive!

Two, because I had this incredible feeling of awe wash over me sitting there on that saddle. I'd just experienced a horse *fully* being a horse. As if he had no rider on his back, because he'd surely forgotten about me 500 hundred yards before. I sat on his back and got to experience what he was made to do. And that feeling of awe overwhelmed me as I closed my eyes and said a quiet prayer of thanks.

I tell this story because I think it's an image of our lives. We get stuck on the trail rides at different times, following the posterior of someone in front of us, as we just try to get through it as fast as possible and make it back home where we can eat and forget that we have to do it all again the next day.

But then there are those moments when we step off the trail and start living the way we were born to live. When everything that held us back, real or imagined, fades away and we just run full-speed, fully alive, not caring any longer who is trying to hold us back.

No one can do what you do or be who you are. Own it. Leverage it. And watch the returns pour in for years to come. Keep changing by becoming more of who you were meant to be.

It's not this self-help search where you feel like you're reading a barely legible treasure map and if you miss some turn, you'll never find your purpose. No, finding your calling involves knowing your gifts, owning your story, getting off the trail, and running as only you can.

I think of Hondo often and the invaluable lesson he taught me that day. And I'm still thankful he didn't have to kill me for me to get the point!

WE DON'T CONNECT
WITH EACH OTHER
THROUGH OUR
PRETEND PERFECTION.
WE CONNECT OVER
OUR SHARED STRUGGLE.
BE BRAVE ENOUGH
TO GO FIRST.

PAUL
ANGONE

101 QUESTIONS
YOU NEED TO ASK
IN YOUR TWENTIES

#101Q

17

What is my "Significant Why"?

Why are you doing what you're doing?

Knowing and defining the "significant why" behind "what" you are pursuing is the most crucial piece to actually accomplishing it.

Your why is what other people will connect to—whether in a job interview, blog article, book, podcast, nonprofit, or business launch.

As Simon Sinek wrote in *Start with Why*, "People don't buy what you do; they buy why you do it."

Yet, all too often we forget our "why." We lose sight of it. Or we just never knew it in the first place.

Not understanding your "why" will leave you directionless. Like standing in the middle of the kitchen, racking your brain as to why you walked in there in the first place.

If you want to do something significant, you must know why it's significant to you.

We have to keep going back to the soul of our motivation, beyond the logistics, the details, making money, or acquiring stuff.

Your why is bigger than you.

I know that more fully now, especially with a wife and three kids. My why is also for them.

YOU MUST KNOW AND OWN YOUR WHY

If your why is at the heart of what you do, the ebbs and flows of the day will not stop you. Sheer success and fantastic failures will not keep you from plugging away.

The weight of your why will break off the doubts and fears that try to hold you back.

Your why will give you the strength to Grit On.

What is your why?

Many of the questions that follow will help you better uncover and define your "significant why."

What are the Pivotal Plot Points of my story?

When reading a book, you don't just open it up for the first time in the middle and expect to understand what's going on with the story.

The same concept applies to your life. You're living a one-of-a-kind story. And if you don't understand your story—where it came from and where it's going—how are you going to effectively live the next pages?

The key is defining, understanding, and articulating, what I call the **Pivotal Plot Points** in your story.

Your Pivotal Plot Points are those key moments in your life where something significant happened—both the good and the bad, the Triumphs and the Tragedies. Understanding the Pivotal Plot Points in your story so far gives you context for where your story is headed because you know where your story has been.

Your past can hold you back from your future or your past can reveal it. Let's pull back the curtain and start better understanding your epic story!

What are the Pivotal Plot Points in your story? Write them down in the following questions.

19

What are 3-5 of my Greatest Triumphs (recognitions, awards, successes, or achievements)?

Write them down below. These can be big, visible successes or they can be intimate achievements that maybe only you know about. Whatever you are truly proud about as your greatest triumphs, write them down.

1.

2.

3.

4.

5.

▲ 20

When have others seen me the most alive?

Sometimes we don't give ourselves credit where it is due because we write off some of our greatest triumphs as no big deal. They *are* a big deal, and sometimes you need someone who is not immersed in the forest to point out some of the trees for you.

Pick 2–3 people closest to you, and ask them when they have seen you come alive the most and experience the most success. You might be surprised what they tell you and what themes emerge. Write down what they say below.

21

When looking at my Greatest Triumphs, what exactly was I doing that felt so meaningful? What need was I meeting?

We all see success differently. What I see as a huge triumph might feel like an everyday experience to you. What *exactly* were you doing that felt so meaningful to you? Were you leading, serving, entertaining, creating, etc.?

In each one of your triumphs, what need were you meeting?

You solved some problem or stepped into a role. You were effectively meeting a need that was extremely satisfying for you.

These needs don't always have to be "solving world hunger" or completely service-related either.

For example, a triumph of mine in college was being master of ceremonies, along with my favorite professor Dr. Greg Spencer, for the biggest school-wide event at my college called *Spring Sing*. Each year, the men and women of every dorm would create full-on musicals and compete against each other to be crowned best of show. Then every year the master of ceremonies was a secret revealed the night of and was a big honor. For months, Dr. Spencer and I worked together to create skits, humorous videos, songs, jokes, etc., that would be placed in between the different dorm productions as we were tasked to keep the show running and the audience engaged for hours. The event was held at the largest concert venue in town as parents flew in and people from the community came to watch.

I definitely had many "freak-out anxiety" moments leading up to the production, and I remember my adrenaline churning full-speed as we waited to step out on the stage in front of a thousand people. Yet, after two and a half hours, I left the stage feeling like the event was a great success, and we received lots of positive affirmation afterwards.

What needs were we meeting as being MCs for a large event? Well, we were meeting a need to entertain, to engage a large audience and keep an event going strong for hours. I can now see within this triumph, many of my strengths and skills that I use today as a speaker and writer as I continually meet the need to entertain and communicate a message effectively for maximum impact. We weren't saving the world that night when Dr. Spencer and I were dressed up as Sonny and Cher singing "I Got You Babe," yet in the context of my story, meeting this need, rising to this challenge and having it turn out really well, was incredibly satisfying and important to me. (And yes, in case you were wondering, I was dressed up as Cher.)

How do you incorporate your Triumphs into your current and

future story? That's the question. Don't lose sight of what you enjoy doing and where you have achieved success in the past because your twenties can get a little murky with perceived failures, failed plans, and expectations going up in flames. Take the Triumphs from your past and incorporate them into your present and future.

Write down what you were doing and the "needs" you were meeting in your biggest triumphs. Are those needs you met in the past possible needs you want to take on in the future?

1.

2.

3.

What are 3-5 of the Greatest Tragedies that I've had to overcome?

Calling these tragedies might sound a bit too Shakespearean, but basically write down some of your biggest perceived failures, accidents, challenges, circumstances, or the hardest seasons of your life that you've had to work through or overcome.

1.

2.

3.

4.

5.

23

What are my problems and personal pain revealing to me about my purpose?

Here's an uplifting question, huh?

This question sounds like it's coming from a psychiatrist who has the strange gift of making you feel *more* depressed about your life than when you first walked into their office. Yes, I unfortunately might be speaking from experience here. The only benefit of seeing that psychiatrist is that, in comparison, he made every moment outside of his office feel like Disneyland. Well, not really. When you're struggling with depression, every day kind of feels like going to Disneyland, paying for tickets, then finding out every ride is broken except for "It's a Small World."

"It's a small world after all . . ."

"Please, no more."

"It's a small world after all . . ."

"No more it's a small world. Please. I beg you . . ."

"It's a small world after all . . ."

"Get me off this boat! I swear I'll swim for it! I don't care if you haven't changed the water since Walt himself took a ride!"

Yet, stay with me, and we'll see how your pain and problems can actually be quite uplifting. I promise. And you can jump off It's a Small World and ride on Space Mountain.

Because here's a powerful truth that I don't think we realize enough in our lives—**oftentimes our purpose and passion is found in our greatest pain.** Your passion and purpose might be embedded in the tragedies you listed above.

I believe God's in the redemption business—taking those broken pieces of our story and creating something breathtaking out of them. **In every great story the hero always experiences an "all is lost" moment before the dramatic rise.**

World changers typically have their greatest impact where they have experienced the most personal pain.

In my own story, for years I felt stuck in a cubicle. I felt frustrated, bitter, and broken. All the big dreams that once burned inside of me began to sizzle out like a sparkler on a summer sidewalk.

I wanted to pursue my purpose and passion, but I began to wonder if the pursuit was pointless. That all this "finding your passion and purpose" talk was in fact a young person's naïveté like so many people paint it to be.

So I began to write.

In a broken down motel room with four locks on the door is where I wrote my first page as I stared at the door and wondered— *why were three locks not enough?*

From that night on, I wrote everywhere I went.

And yet for most of that first year writing, I didn't even know what I was writing about.

So I wrote about the struggle. I wrote about the unanswered questions. I wrote about the frustration, the problems I was facing that I didn't have an answer for.

That's when it began to happen. I began to find my purpose in the least expected place. And no, it was not during my two and a half sessions with the most depressing psychiatrist ever who not-so-ironically claimed he specialized in helping depression.

I began to find my purpose in my biggest problems.

As I stared at my biggest questions and frustrations about trying to find my purpose, passion, and place in my twenties, and I failed to find any simple answers, a passion began to boil within me to help others who must be experiencing the same problems.

Through this lonely struggle, I found my "significant why"—empowering my generation, and those leading it, with overwhelming amounts of truth, hope, and hilarity as we inspire and save each other from living a ho-hum "groan up" life.

My *why* was forged in failure. My *why* became bigger than me. Bigger than all the noes I received from publishers and all the setbacks. Because my why was as serious to me as life or death. I knew what it was like to be desperately searching for hope, and I wanted to help others on that same journey.

Failure doesn't ruin your story. Failure helps you write it.

Your why might be birthed from the same place. Failed plans. Heartbreak. Pain. Frustration. Setbacks. Unmet expectations.

Rarely is your *why* birthed in the spotlight.

You see this idea played out in most of the greatest inventions, movements, and social changes throughout history.

The most significant achievements typically aren't birthed out of inspiration; they are squeezed out by necessity.

When you've experienced a pain and frustration so intense, you bring that same intensity to finding a solution, a better way.

Because the problem is not theoretical for you. No, the problem has held your head underwater, and you know the fight that it took to just catch a breath.

So if you're struggling to find your purpose and passion, look to your problems. Look at those tragedies you've experienced and see what is waiting there to be redeemed.

Your passion is driven by the deep desire to solve a deep need.

Your struggles aren't a distraction from your calling; sometimes your struggles are the pathway to it.

You need the struggle to infuse in you the grit, perseverance, and empathy it takes to produce change.

THE GIFT OF PROBLEMS

Your biggest problems might be your purpose waiting to be unwrapped.

Look at your pain, and you might find purpose waiting there with a slight, knowing smirk.

So the question becomes: what is something (birthed out of the tragedies of your own story) that breaks your heart or is a big need you want to do something about?

What injustice or problems make you angrier than a parrot being poked with a stick?

Knowing what breaks your heart can clarify what makes you feel whole.

And then, here's the real kicker—what's something you can do about it right now, big or small?

Write down what makes you frustrated, breaks your heart, or is simply a problem you'd like to find an answer for. If nothing else, thinking about our problems and pain in this way helps us step off of It's a Small World before we have to swim for it.

1.

2.

3.

Outside of my Tragedies and Triumphs, what are some other needs that I am passionate about?

Are there other ways to spot needs that don't necessarily come out of your triumphs or tragedies that you might want to do something about? Here are some different ways to spot more needs.

• **Look at the World**

When you look at the world you live in, what frustrates you, or what problems would you love to address?

a. On a macro level (big picture)?

b. On a micro level (your community, church, family)?

• Look at Your Work or School Environment

What have you been complaining about at work or at school? Write down a few of your biggest frustrations.

How can you enter into that complaint, which is typically because you see a problem, with a solution? Brainstorm here:

What do you find yourself reading the most about—politics, social justice, family issues, parenting tips, designing better websites? Write some of those down.

25

ADVLT

Instead of trying
to solve life's big
problems late
at night as an
anxious exhaustion
swallows me like
a black fog, should
I try something
more productive,
like, you know,
going to sleep?
The morning is
magnificently
redemptive.

26

How do I keep doing inspiring work even when I feel completely uninspired?

Receiving jolts of inspiration is amazing.

I love when a movie, song, friend, picture, or place picks me up and breathes life into my soul. Or one of the biggest pick-me-ups, when a reader reaches out to me or I meet someone at a speaking engagement who tells me how much something I wrote impacted them. After receiving kind words like that, I pretty much float over my computer while I write for at least an hour.

Yet, inspiration is like caffeine. No matter how much I take in, at some point it wears off. Most of the time with a giant crash that leaves me feeling worse off than before I started.

How do we keep doing inspiring work even when we feel completely uninspired? How do we push through the negativity and self-doubt to keep doing the work we need to do? Well, on a farm in the middle of Kansas, I think I found the answer.

MY GREAT-UNCLE RUSSELL'S FARM

Recently, I went on a mission to find and resurrect my grandfather's old '75 Ford pickup truck, which had been sitting dormant in a barn in Kansas at my great-uncle's farm for seven years.

As a kid, I loved riding with my grandpa across the back roads of Kansas inside that pickup truck, as we made our way to our favorite fishing pond at my great-uncle's farm. Driving on a two-lane highway, as my grandpa passed old farmers driving their old pickup trucks, I always marveled as both men would raise their hands off their steering wheel at each other in a friendly wave. It was like all these old farmers and trucks were a part of the same secret club that I wished I could be a part of too.

My grandpa and great-uncle have since moved on from this life years ago. I still miss them both very much. And whenever I'd think about them, I'd think about that old Ford pickup truck. Where was it? Did it still run? I had no idea where the truck was, but I knew I needed to find it.

I felt like there was part of my story wrapped up in that old pickup truck. Something about the farm, the truck, the hard work, and memories of my grandfather and great-uncle, compelled me to find and hopefully bring the truck home even though I didn't really know if it was even possible.

Thankfully, I was able to connect with my amazing cousins who lived on or near my great-uncle's farm, and they had my grandpa's old pickup truck in a barn. And it was mine if I was willing to come drag it out!

I enlisted my brother's help, and together we took off on a crazy rescue mission. When we got to the farm and pulled open the barn doors, seeing that red-and-white Ford from my childhood was a thing of beauty. All beat up and rusty, with the driver's side door barely able to open and close because the truck had rolled down a hill and into a wood post while my great-uncle stopped to feed his cows. I loved every inch of it! Every dent and the story it told.

As I explored my great-uncle's farm that I grew up coming to as a kid, I was reminded of the answer to the question I asked above. I was shown the secret to doing amazing and inspiring work. As I looked at the work he'd accomplished over his lifetime, it all became very clear to me.

The secret to doing amazing work—

Keep showing up.

Keep working the ground.

Keep grinding. Keep planting. Keep watering. Keep building.

As you might have heard me say before (and I need to remind myself of daily)—

Sometimes the most inspired thing you can do is to keep showing up when you feel completely uninspired.

As I look around my great-uncle's farm and see what he built, it's one amazing accomplishment after another.

No fanfare. No frills. Just consistent, quality, *everydayness.*

He would work hard. Make progress. And then a tornado would hit the farm (actually three tornadoes, three different times, according to my cousin).

Or something would break down. Or it wouldn't rain.

Yet, no matter the circumstances, he never stopped doing what he knew he needed to do.

Find another way. Keep working the problem. Keep showing up.

Do amazing work by continually doing the work.

Yes, we can strive to live an inspiring life and need to find ways to keep feeding our soul. Yet, I think most successful people aren't on a desperate search for inspiration so that they can do the work. I think successful people do the work first, and then the inspiration follows.

Pursuing your dreams isn't mythical, it's methodic.

Your twenties are not about what you harvest, but what you plant in the ground. **Pursuing a dream is like planting an avocado seed. It will probably take about seven years before you see any fruit.**

If my great-uncle had let motivation and inspiration prompt his work, there would be no farm there today.

An amazing mechanic in McPherson, Kansas, stayed at his shop until 10:30 p.m. to help us get the truck back on the road. He knew we were going to attempt the ten-hour drive back to Colorado. As he pointed to different things in the engine that possibly could go wrong, he paused and said,

"I can't say this with 100 percent certainty, but I think you'll make it home."

A fitting line for our twenties (and thirties).

As I drove back to Colorado in my grandpa's truck for the first time, smiling from ear to ear as I weaved down old, country two-lane highways, an amazing and unexpected thing began to happen.

As I passed the old farmers in their beat-up trucks, they lifted their hand off the steering wheel and waved at me. And I happily waved back. I was now part of the club. I think I smiled all the way home, which we unbelievably made it to without any problems whatsoever. This old truck that hadn't run in seven years plowed through the 400-mile drive like it was fresh off the lot.

Every time I look at the truck now, I see my grandpa and great-uncle. I see the farm. Every time I drive by an old farmer and I get a wave, it's all one big reminder. Keep doing the work. If I don't, they'll kick me out of the club.

27

Am I trying to kill a rat in my life by taking the rat poison myself?

Man, being bitter just feels so right sometimes, doesn't it?

When by all accounts and witnesses you have every right to be utterly furious with someone, yet as you replay all the wrongs like a Spice Girls song stuck in your head, the more you play it over and over, the worse and worse you feel.

You have every right *not* to forgive, yet holding tight to that anger is like letting that person repeat the offense over and over—completely tearing you apart while doing nothing to affect them. As author Anne Lamott describes best:

"Not forgiving is like drinking rat poison and then waiting for the rat to die."

Now hear me, I don't know your situation. I don't know the stuff you've been subjected to. Yet, forgiveness is more for you than it is for the person you're forgiving. It allows you to be free and move forward.

Forgiveness rarely happens overnight. In my life, forgiveness has been a process that's taken a lot of prayer and some counseling. And it's not easy.

Unforgiveness is like hitching a big box TV to your ankle and then trying to run uphill. Unhitch it and never look back. Unforgiveness is a weight that is too heavy to carry.

Forgiveness means stopping the bitterness and resentment from continually seeping into your heart like a gas leak. Forgiveness means when your mind starts replaying the offenses in your head, and you dream about all the things you wish you would have said or done to them in return, you stop the reenactment. You change your thoughts. You let your "right" to be angry go.

For me, that usually means praying to God for help. Every time I visualize wanting to punch that other person in the face, asking God to take the anger away from me.

It's not easy. It's not simple. But it's better than taking the rat poison yourself and then going online and combing through the rat's recent vacation photos to Hawaii.

ALL EXPLORERS HAVE TO FIRST

GET

LOST

28

Depending on how we use it, social media can feel like attending a bad high school party where everyone is staring at you, not saying a word. Or it can be something more meaningful. On a scale of 1-10, how would I rank my online social networking?

Back in the day, you had to go to your ten-year high school re-union to see who was doing better than who. And you just had to fake it for one night.

Buy a new outfit that looks like money (that you're returning the next day to get all that money back). Rent the BMW. Rent a spouse. Rent some kids. Whatever it takes. Just play the part for three hours, then that night you could be nestled back in your tailor-made imprint on your parents' couch, eating the fifth slice from your Little Caesar's pizza that you've covered in ranch dressing. You successfully crafted your success like a Las Vegas magician and can peacefully continue your real life for ten more years.

However, with the invention of social media, we're now trying to pull off that same magic show every single day. Every picture, every post, every exciting announcement, is a reminder to everyone about how amazing our lives really are! It's exhausting. Our Obsessive Comparison Disorder running wild like a lion that escaped from the zoo. Dangerous, ravenous, with no clue where we're going.

Yet, there can be power and purpose to social media. I know that firsthand. I would not be a published author today without social media. Pinterest of all places literally changed my life as my article "21 Secrets For Your Twenties" spread like wildfire with beautiful people like yourself pinning the article on their Pinterest boards. (Seriously, you look amazing today. Did you do something different with your hair?)

So is social media the number one cause of Obsessive Comparison Disorder? Or is it an amazing means to reach an audience and find your community in ways we never could've attempted before? Well, it's both. Just like any tool, its effectiveness depends on how you use it.

Either social media is a black hole, sucking all your time, energy, and creativity into a vortex of zero returns.

Or social media can create a galaxy of opportunities, relationships, and platforms like never seen before.

Social media is the great amplifier, shouting the good and bad of YOU at record octaves. It takes your successes, failures, fears, and puts them on stage for the world to judge. And how you're presenting yourself on the social media stage can make all the difference.

So the real question here is—

Are you intentionally or unintentionally doing online social networking?

Is your social media presence proactive or reactive?

Are you strategically creating your online brand or are you letting others create the brand for you?

I think the most powerful combo is being authentic on social media, while also being strategic to your long-term goals. A strategic authenticity might sound like an inauthentic paradox, but I think it's possible. It's maintaining consistency between your digital and physical selves. Striving to be the best, most honest version of yourself, in both worlds.

Social media is like a chainsaw. How you wield it is the difference between actually building something. Or just cutting everything down.

Can I laugh at myself?

More and more I'm coming to the realization that our ability to do great things hinges on our ability to laugh at ourselves, especially in our twenties when everything feels like a grand mystery and mistakes are as prevalent as all your college debt (still paying off mine!).

And my wife would probably be the first to tell you that I am, without a doubt, terrible at laughing at myself! Truly. How bad I am at laughing at myself is no laughing matter.

It's really quite remarkable. I make a mistake. I defensively defend that mistake to convince everyone it was not a mistake. I get angry that no one is listening to my defense that doesn't make sense. Then I want to storm out and throw a big rock at another rock. Or something like that.

I know I need to continue cultivating the skill of laughing at myself. The ability to leave mistakes right where they are and not carry them with you like a bag of underfed snapping turtles.

I will make mistakes. You will make mistakes. You are not your mistakes. There will be more mistakes. But the biggest mistake of all would be to not see the humorous side to them, learn from them, and then let those mistakes go.

The ability to laugh at yourself is like letting mistakes sail out to sea, instead of tying them around your torso as they try to drag you to the bottom.

Marriage is like driving a car. Even if you're in the front seat, it doesn't mean you understand what's going on under the hood. Why do some people have great marriages while others have complete wrecks before they even make it to the highway?

We all have ideas of what a healthy marriage should be, but I'd argue some of these expectations are unhealthy myths. **It's these myths about marriage that mess marriage up before your marriage can even happen.**

Whether you're happy and single, seriously dating, or already married, busting some of these marriage myths can be the difference between being happily married or looking for a way out.

5 MYTHS ABOUT MARRIAGE

Myth #1 – Married People Know What They're Doing

In my single days, I'd go to a wedding and think, "Wow, there's two people who have it all figured out."

Then I got married and realized pretty quickly that I didn't have a clue.

As I wrote in *101 Secrets For Your Twenties*, "Marriage in your 20s can feel a lot like playing House."

There's no textbook for husband and wife, no matter what new bestselling book tries to convince you otherwise.

Marriage doesn't just define you, you also define it.

If it feels like you're playing House, it's because there should be healthy amounts of exploration, creativity, and unknowns in marriage. That's normal.

You grow into growing up as your roots grow deeper together. **Marriage doesn't just happen at your wedding. Marriage develops slowly during the thousands of days thereafter.**

Myth #2 – Your Spouse Is Your Best Friend

Yes, I do believe your spouse should be the closest friend you've ever had. If friendship isn't your foundation, when those first waves hit, your relationship's sexy wall décor will be floating out to sea.

Yet, many of us are determined to make our spouse our best friend, which really means trying to mold and mash our spouse into acting the way we think a best friend should be.

Keep your best friends your best friends.

Make the friendship with your spouse into an elite category of its own. Not solely based on your perspective and previous experience of what a best friend should be, but on what works for both of you.

Stop trying to reprint with your partner what you think a best friend looks like and start painting a new picture together.

"YOUR WIFE MIGHT NOT TELL JOKES LIKE YOUR COLLEGE ROOMMATE DID. YOUR HUSBAND MIGHT NOT TALK FOR HOURS INTO THE NIGHT LIKE YOUR BEST FRIEND FROM HOME. THAT'S ALL RIGHT. LIKE DRINKING WINE OR A CUP OF COFFEE, THEY BOTH MIGHT TASTE DELICIOUS, BUT EACH WILL HAVE AN ENTIRELY DIFFERENT FLAVOR."

– 101 Secrets For Your Twenties

Myth #3 – Marriage Completes You

Your spouse is not God, a magic genie, or a unicorn with wish-granting abilities. Your spouse is a human.

If you're putting unrealistic mythical expectations on your relationship, it might end up more Greek tragedy than romantic comedy.

A good relationship should not complete you. No, it should inspire you daily to work on your incompleteness.

Myth #4 – Whom You Choose to Marry Is the Most Important Choice You'll Ever Make.

Choosing your spouse is extremely important. Choosing your spouse every day after the wedding is even more so.

Marriages don't just explode, they slowly unravel.

Day by day, life and time and to-dos and struggles and hurts and strains and bad habits left untouched create rifts that grow over time.

There are so many moments throughout the day when you have a choice to choose your spouse. Or not.

When you have a computer in front of you. When you start flirting with that coworker. When you just consistently choose to stay at work a little later every night. When you feel bitterness and anger creeping into your heart yet don't address it.

Marriages don't fall apart because of one big compromise. They fall apart due to a thousand small ones. Like a windshield crack, the longer you drive on without addressing the issue, the more shattered your relationship will become.

Myth #5 – Marriage is a One-Time Thing

One of my mentors loves saying that he's been married seven times to the same woman.

I never understood what he meant when I was single. Now, I get it.

Marriage is not static. It's not a one-size-fits-all pair of jeans that will always wear the exact same. Your relationship will change because people change.

In marriage, you have to be willing to readjust and recommit to new seasons. Sometimes that change is screaming in your face (aka a newborn). And sometimes the change is more subtle and nuanced. It could be a promotion, a death, new life, or a new city.

We have to adapt and grow as people, and so do our relationships.

The conditions in your marriage may change, but your commitment should not.

Do you work hard and are you easy to work with?

Late night TV show host Conan O'Brien is not just for laughs—although he brings those in droves in his own witty, self-deprecating style. The Harvard grad is also incredibly smart and strikes me as a humble guy who honestly enjoys helping people.

I watched a town hall discussion Conan did with the students at Harvard, and when a student asked him how he could set himself apart in his career against the competition, this was Conan's advice: work hard, and be easy to work with.

So simple. So true. Yet as Conan so poignantly put, "You put those two things together and, in any economy, sadly you'll be a rarity."

32

ADULT

Am I being brave enough to be awkward?

Do I ever allow myself to just be awkward?

We are killing awkward. And the effects might be killing us.

Awkward silence. Awkward conversations. Awkward waiting. All becoming a thing of the past.

Long line at the grocery aisle? Let me take out my phone.

Long drive? Let me blare some music.

Long ride up an elevator? Please Lord let my phone pick up some sort of 4G . . . or even 3G . . . just any G so that I can pretend I don't see the person awkwardly standing next to me.

Long flight? Gosh I hope the plane has Wi-Fi and a good movie! Those dreaded ten minutes where they make you turn off your electronic devices, the scariest part of flying 30,000 feet in the air.

Because . . .

Silence is deafening . . . scary . . . and awkward.

We no longer live annoyed by distractions. We live for them.

Why?

Is it because when we're alone and silent, we actually have to think about our lives? The good, the bad, and the awkward?

I obsessively check email, hoping to see something new when I can't keep up with the emails already there.

The iPhone is our generation's cigarette. We are the Refresh Generation—constantly getting a hit from our phone for the latest update. Too many of us are chain-smoking our phones. **Is there an e-patch?**

We crave the distraction. The busyness. We are addicted to being notified by the immediate. It makes us feel important to be wrapped up in the frenzy.

Yet is this healthy?

THE ILL EFFECTS OF NONSTOPNESS

We have killed awkward and the effects are killing us.

Experts say the *constantness* of our culture heightens heart disease, dementia, and early death.

We need silence. For our mind to have the freedom to let itself wander. To stumble upon those unexpected surprises that only come through being comfortable to exist in the uncomfortable.

Our days pre-technology used to be filled with awkward moments. Of silence. Of space. Where we allowed the possibility for a feeling or a thought to fill it—whether good or bad. Now we run from both. Maybe you are not having any breakthrough ideas because you don't give your mind any time and space to think about them.

When we remove all awkward, we remove all possibilities for unexpected amazing.

This question is more of a challenge than anything else. Today I challenge you when you start feeling awkward and feel the pull to go for your phone or music to block it, stop yourself. And just sit and be awkward. You might be surprised what awkward and amazing discoveries come your way.

Be brave enough to be awkward.

How do I stop networking and start "relationshipping"?

Networking events feel like going to prom all over again, except you didn't even come with a date this time. And you might be feeling even more self-conscious than you did at seventeen. (I didn't believe this was possible either!)

My palms get sweaty just thinking about stepping into that loud room where everyone seems to know each other, my main goal, just like prom—not to make a fool of myself.

But you can't act too shy because you have about three minutes before the Business Card Slinger smells your fear from across the room and has you signed up for his "can't miss opportunity" before you even have a chance to say your name.

For so many years I avoided "networking" opportunities like I avoided going to the pool as a teenager.

But then I realized I had networking all wrong. And I believe for many of us our "networking" attempts are actually having a negative effect on our job search, career building, and entrepreneurial efforts.

Many of us have seen the stats that an estimated 70–80% of all job opportunities come through relationships, which I totally agree with.

But let's stop networking to make it happen.

Let's start *relationshipping* instead. When I switched from networking to relationshipping, it changed everything for me.

If you stop networking and start relationshipping, I can guarantee better job openings, career growth, and opportunities than you've ever experienced before. Also, you won't feel like you're walking into a room in your swimsuit trying to convince everyone that you were once a runway model.

Stop networking like a machine. Start relationshipping like a person.

Okay, so what does relationshipping actually look like, and how do we do it well?

How do I do relationshipping better?

Here are some ideas for better relationshipping that will change the way you meet people and allow you make deeper, more meaningful connections than any networking tactic will do.

7 IDEAS FOR BETTER RELATIONSHIPPING

1. Build new relationships when you don't "need" them.

We typically network when we need something. Then all too often we become *that guy* who's roaming through the halls giving off that nervous tinge of desperation. And the moment there is a lull in conversation he thrusts his business card in there like a dead rat.

Don't be that guy.

Start implementing a practice and habit of getting to know new people, even when you have no specific "need" to do so.

That's the hardest part about networking—typically only doing it when we desperately need a door to open for us. Instead, cultivate the life habit of seeking a new person out every week and getting to know their story.

Here's an example of the amazing things that can happen when you're open to meet new people wherever you are. This happened for me on a plane ride a couple months after my first book *101 Secrets For Your Twenties* was released. I wasn't "needing" to meet someone, yet the three of us in my row ended up talking to each other the whole trip. By the end of trip, the female passenger was so encouraged and intrigued by my work writing to twentysomethings that she pretty much told me that I was now going to have lunch with her boyfriend because she felt we needed to talk.

Long story short, her boyfriend was a well-connected Hollywood manager for actors, actresses, and writers, we hit it off, and he was soon shopping *101 Secrets For Your Twenties* around to be made into a TV sitcom. Crazy!

Then as well, he invited me to a gathering at his house where some various people were going to be recording music demos in his basement recording studio. This had **Awkward Hollywood Experience** written all over it. I knew I was going to feel more out of place than a horse trying to dip a chip at the salsa bar. And yet, I went.

I ended up finding a safe corner of the house where I had a great conversation with a gal named Sasha. She was there to record some songs so we talked a lot about music, writing, etc. Afterwards, my manager was very excited that I'd connected so well with her.

"Dude! Great job connecting with Sasha. We need to send her a copy of *101 Secrets For Your Twenties*!"

"Okay, sounds great. Yeah I enjoyed talking to her," I said, not quite understanding what he was getting at. My manager then mentioned something about Sasha actually being more of an actress than a singer. He mentioned some TV show, which of course I played off like I knew what he was talking about, hoping I could at least understand one word he was saying so Google could explain it to me later.

Well, it didn't take much Googling to figure out that Sasha Pieterse was on the TV show "Pretty Little Liars," which I learned was a pretty popular show. And two days later I would wake up to my phone almost short-circuiting because Sasha shared an image of *101 Secrets For Your Twenties* on her Instagram, and even a few lines from the book on Twitter, to her millions and millions of followers. Years later, I still have teenage girls tweeting me, asking if I can introduce them to Sasha.

All because I didn't put my headphones on and block everyone out on the plane ride that day.

2. Be about them for the first 10 minutes.

I have a good friend who I consider a master conversationalist. He's someone you can't wait to speak to and be around. And if I had to boil down his secret conversational sauce to just one thing, I would say he's just really good at being excited about the person in front of him.

When I asked him for his secret to being so good at conversations, he told me that when he goes into a conversation he intentionally tries to have the person in front of him talk first for at least ten minutes before he says anything about himself.

Stop parachuting into conversations and holding every minute hostage with all the things you're passionate about.

Instead, start getting excited about all the things the person across from you is passionate about. **Your excitement about them will make them much more excited about you.**

3. Check in on people.

Send a text. A quick email. Make a call. Check in on people. In our hyperactive social world, the intentional "wanted to see how you are doing" message with no favor to ask at the end can go a long way to building a strong relationship.

4. Give real, meaningful compliments.

The most powerful relationshipping tool you have is a well-placed, meaningful compliment.

When reaching out to fellow alumni from your school. When asking to write a guest post for your favorite website. When trying to connect with someone through Twitter or LinkedIn.

Lead with real compliments.

No matter how big of a deal a person is, they will pay attention to someone who has noticed their work and has something nice to say about it.

Not a fake, cliché, general compliment about them being "amazing." It needs to be something specific.

Do some research. Find an article they've written. Study a project they were involved in. Find a recent promotion on LinkedIn.

Don't shout *at* a person, shout about how cool that person is.

The real power of social media is complimenting others instead of yourself.

Bonus Tip: Please for the love of humanity, when you're trying to connect with someone through email, lead with their name. I can't tell you how many emails I get from people who say they love my site and want to write for it, or want me to check out their work and give them feedback, but they never actually use my name in the email. And they never actually say my website name "All Groan Up." This screams to me spam, stock email you're firing out to as many people as you can find. *Holster that email, cowboy, before you start hurting people.*

5. Be present.

Every time you stare at your phone across from someone you're supposed to be talking with, you're telling them that your phone is more important than they are.

6. Be a connector.

Think of two people in your life right now who don't know each other, but would benefit from connecting with the other. Send a quick email connecting the two, with specific, meaningful compliments about both people. Now you've just accomplished a 2 for 1, deepening your connection with both people as you also help them out with their connections.

7. How can you help them?

Find out what they're struggling with and start offering solutions, assistance, and service. "I'd love to help you . . ." "I've got an idea that might help with this problem . . ."

Relationshipping is about serving others instead of serving yourself. It's not only more helpful and meaningful for them, but it's a thousand times more effective for you as well.

35

ADULT

How do I combat my anxiety?

Worry crushes creativity.

Worry warps wisdom.

Worry pummels peace.

We must wreck worry before it wrecks us. But how?

I'm going to make two arguments about anxiety here.

First, an important part to combating your anxiety is defining it.

Second, maybe some of your anxiety can actually be a good thing.

Let me explain.

FIRST, COMBATING ANXIETY

The most important part to combating your anxiety is what I call DYA—Define Your Anxiety.

My wife, Naomi, and I talk about this often and how much it helps our mental state when we stop anxiety before it can run amok in our house and we figure out its name.

I believe we feel the most anxious when it's nameless. When it's faceless. When it's this ambiguous, looming fear that we feel is ready to strike, yet we have no idea from where or why.

When we stop and define the anxiety, we are able to better strategize how to remove that fear or lie from our life. Fighting against anxiety is not an easy, straightforward process, but figuring out exactly what we're battling against is the first important step.

And secondly . . .

What is my anxiety telling me?

Sometimes I think it can really be a good thing that you're feeling anxious!

If you weren't feeling anxious, then I'd be worried! Because your anxiety is telling you something really important, if you'll listen.

Anxiety is either lying to you or it's telling you the exact truth. In the moment, it's vital you know which one it is.

Let me explain.

For example, you're at a store when you spot a beautiful necklace that you just have to buy. But you look at the price tag—$75! That's highway robbery. And without really thinking about it, you do something completely abnormal for you—you slip the necklace in your pocket and walk out of the store.

As you drive away, the adrenaline wears off as another feeling overwhelmingly takes its place. *Anxiety.*

What the heck did I just do? That's not the kind of person I am.

I'd argue this is not an anxiety stemming from a lie or fear, but an anxiety produced by conviction. And in those cases, anxiety has a lot of productive things to tell you. In this instance, your anxiety is telling you the truth.

So the answer to some anxiety doesn't come from defining it and trying to relieve the anxiety by having more faith and counteracting it with truth.

Sometimes the anxiety is pointing to the truth and you only relieve the anxiety by doing something that your anxiety is screaming at you that you need to do. It's an anxiety produced from conviction that is telling you to make a change *or else*.

Maybe you've noticed that after watching a couple hours of your favorite TV show, you've begun to feel anxious. Maybe that anxiety is not something to squash by itself, rather it's telling you that you're wasting too much time watching TV. You don't relieve the anxiety by watching more TV. You watch less TV, which then helps relieve your anxiety.

Define your anxiety. Listen to it. Then either kick the anxiety out with the opposite truth or hear the truth and make a change.

DO IT BIG.
DO IT SMALL.

JUST DO SOMETHING.

Marriage is like rolling Play-Doh; the more two different colors are mashed together the harder it becomes to distinguish one from the other. *Do I want to become mashed together for life with the person I'm dating (or hoping to date)?*

In marriage you begin to rub off on each other, subtly taking on traits and characteristics of the other.

Does this thought excite you or does it make you feel like you just digested a can of the aforementioned Play-Doh?

Yes in marriage you still are your own person. And you need to have your own identity beyond your spouse.

However . . .

If you don't want to become like the person you're dating, well, then should you really be dating?

38 ◆

Do I see that finding someone attractive is much more profound and complex than just thinking they're smoking hot?

One of the biggest lies of our culture is that attraction is solely about appearance. We gawk at the sexy, celebrity marriages, yet sometimes these marriages last about 3/4ths of the way down the aisle, when the groom asks for a bridesmaid's number.

In our culture, we act like if you can just get your hair, abs, complexion, and clothes just right, then *The One* will scamper to you like a squirrel to a nut factory. Then when the squirrel doesn't stay for more than two weeks, we sit in disbelief with a slight smirk on our face—mainly because we've had so much Botox we couldn't frown if we wanted to.

Why don't we talk about the fact that attraction runs much deeper than looks? Sure appearance might catch someone's eye, but it's personality, values, faith, heart, and your past, present, and future story that's going to make them stay.

What is love?

Wow, could I possibly ask a broader, more insightful question? While I'm at it why don't I just ask—why is the sky blue? Where do babies come from? And why are bushes bushy? Or how do you fold a fitted sheet? Oh wait, that is a good question. *How do you?*

Yet, no other word in human language has been misconstrued, mistrusted, celebrated, worshiped, and cursed more than love.

We all want love, right? But do we have any clue what love really is?

One thing many of us know about love—it has let us down. Love has *Indiana Jones'd* our heart, ripping it out without even putting us under.

Love cures us and makes us sick, sometimes in the same look.

What is love? How do we get it? And how do we keep it?

To answer these questions, we need to first figure out what love *is not*. We need to remove some lies we believe about love to get down to the core of what love really is.

1. LOVE IS NOT EFFORTLESS.

The movies make it look like love should be effortless and easygoing, when marriage requires more effort and intentionality than you ever knew you had.

My wife and I are ten years and three kids into our relationship, and I would say that this past year has been the most intense yet.

Not a bad year. But a really good, bonding, breaking, yet building one.

I think mainly this year has taught my wife and me that sometimes being in love means fighting *for* each other.

Not a polite, politically correct little skirmish either. No, an all-out, gloves off, *doing whatever it takes* brawl against all the forces, distractions, bad habits, and complexities that try to break our love.

Love is war. Not against one another, but for each other.

In a relationship, you have to fight against everything that is trying to keep you fighting.

And that might be waging war on your own faults and insecurities that you've tried to pretend don't exist.

Sometimes the most loving thing you can do is get on your knees in the muck and mud and start pulling the weeds that are trying to keep your love from reaching its full potential.

You have to work the hardest for who and what you love the most.

2. LOVE IS NOT SEX.

Somehow love and sex have been intertwined like a pretzel. But trying to make love equal sex will only leave you flat on your face.

Call me your Great Uncle Ed, but we're giving away sex these days like free Pop-Tarts—buying, heating, and consuming in less than a minute and a half.

Sex is not love. No, for many of us, sex has become the easiest escape from love and the biggest block to receiving love. Easing all our insecurities, fears, and pains into a moment of escape that does nothing to alleviate our pain. No, most likely it only heightens the pain once the deed is done.

Sex can be a liar. It can prop up an intimacy that has no foundation to sustain it. Letting physical intimacy run wild and free typically means the emotional, spiritual, and personality attraction is lagging behind. And unsuccessfully trying to catch up.

If you've had sex with the person you're dating, I'm not saying it's over and you can't love each other. But what I am saying is that sex while dating can create many awful shades of gray, when what your relationship needs is some honest black and white.

Sex is an amazing expression of committed love, not the pathway to it.

3. LOVE IS NOT SELF-SUSTAINABLE.

Love cannot exist purely within your own convenience. Love is sacrifice.

Some of us want love to just happen on our own terms. In our timing. Under our conditions and if it doesn't interfere with our plans.

Love is not self-sustainable. It can't run well unless you're putting in the right fuel and taking care of it.

This year especially, my wife and I have had to learn a whole new translation of what it means to sustain love.

When a one year old is crying in the middle of the night, and you get up even though it's your partner's turn—that's love.

When you're willing to sit down and look each other in the eyes and have an honest, (mostly) calm conversation about ways you could be supporting each other better—that's love.

Love is a dance where both partners lead and follow throughout the song. Both partners supporting each other's weight, moving with each other's rhythm. With each other's step.

When one person pushes or pulls too hard, the whole dance topples.

Should I be asking— "Is life fair?"

Why is life not fair?

If I wrote a book called *101 Questions You Need to Stop Asking Yourself in Your Twenties*, "why is life not fair?" would be top on the list. Next to questions like—"How do I YOLO more today?" and "What's the most effective way to complain on social media?"

Yet, I know I am constantly struggling with this internal struggle of "why is life not fair." This struggle is birthed from my Obsessive Comparison Disorder, my whole concept of fairness stemming from the perceived ease of life or sheer success of someone else.

And every day I get to see this fun little battle of fairness play out with my two daughters, who are currently six and four years old. For example, they both ask for a blueberry muffin. I try to put up a small fatherly defense of "Dinner is coming soon" or "Didn't you just eat a piece of cinnamon raisin bread, isn't this the same thing?" but being that it's 3:00 p.m. and I'm beginning to hit that caffeine crash, they can smell victory. So they pester and say please and give me a hug, and basically pull out every trick in their arsenal. So finally I say yes. But since the muffins are quite large, and to save some fatherly pride that I'm not a complete pushover, I compromise that they each get half a muffin.

They jump with excitement. They've heard they're getting muffins and a cheer of sheer joy arises from these two little beautiful songbirds bouncing across the floor.

I quickly split the muffins, put a half on each plate, and put it on the table. These two girls have just desperately pleaded their case for their need of a muffin. They have struggled, they have strategized, and they have succeeded. Is their first response to the muffin placed before them more joy as they dive in to take that first succulent bite?

Nope. They sit down and each head turns toward the other plate, and they both say in unison, "Dad, why did she get more than me!"

We are born with this weird, strange Fairness Fluxometer, constantly comparing and gauging the gifts in front of us with the gifts sitting in front of others.

"Why is life not fair?"

The answer to this question is simple. Life is never fair. Or maybe life is always fair. It's a question of perspective more than anything else.

Instead of focusing on the things I don't have, how can I find contentment in all the things I do? How do I see that even the challenges and struggles I'm going through right now are extremely important and good?

Life is not about a question of fairness, but a question of our attitude in regards to the perceived fairness or lack thereof.

Let's just eat the muffin in front of us and be content, instead of worrying about "their" muffin being bigger and better.

Where's the future of work headed, and what does having a successful career look like?

I don't think career success and career growth look the same any more. In the past, it was described as a linear climb going up the corporate ladder or climbing the stairs to get to the top where your corner office and big salary were waiting for you.

In today and tomorrow's economy, I think this will be less and less the reality of what achieving career success will look like. I just gave a keynote talk at a tech conference about the future of work and the keys to engaging, leading, and retaining the digital work-force. To prepare for the talk, I did a deep dive into books like *Big Data*, *The Second Machine Age*, and *The Industries of the Future*, putting together patterns and trends on what it's going to take for companies to be successful in the future with the Millennial gen-eration as well as Gen Z, but also what it's going to take for us and future generations to thrive in an increasingly technological age.

While I came to many conclusions, here is the main key for us to thrive in today and tomorrow's economy:

We need to be excellent tinkers and thinkers in the intangibles.

Yes, we still need to be able to use the technologies and tools in front of us, and companies need to provide the best tools to stay competitive, yet we need be able to venture into the unknowns, into the questions, and be able to pull out patterns, insights, and conclusions that aren't necessarily obvious.

Machines are really good at figuring out the "what" as they extrapolate data. They don't yet excel at understanding, comprehending, and communicating the "why."

Machines can't ask good questions. We can.

Again, this is why it is so important for you to own and hone your unique Signature Sauce, bringing together different insights and experiences that no one, or no machine, can. This is why going through this book and answering some of these questions is so crucial to your success now and for the future. Ask yourself good questions so that you can ask others even better ones.

As machines continually make work more automated, we need to be able to think of ideas that create something new. As technologies become better we need to become better humans.

We need to become creative mashups who can create creative mashups.

THE CAREER JOURNEY

I think the career path for many twentysomethings will look less like a climb and more like a journey, exploring from job-island to job-island, picking up necessary skills and resources at each stop before exploring further.

I created the Career Journey diagram below that I feel represents a more accurate picture of what a "career path" looks like today and tomorrow. As you look at your own job experiences, skill-set growth, and unique Signature Sauce, fill in the diagram below with your most meaningful work/volunteer experiences and then what specific skills you gained on that stop. Then at the very bottom of the diagram in the "Skill Set Promise Land," place those skills you most want to incorporate into your future work.

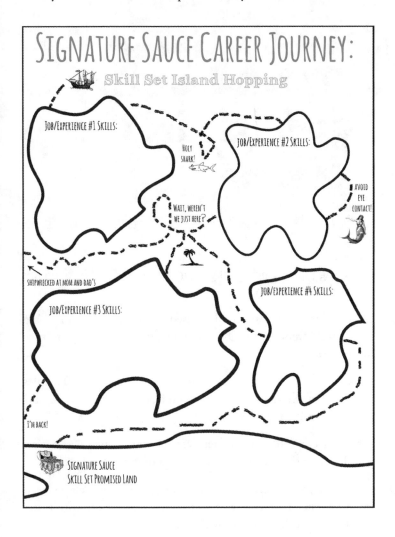

42

Am I dreaming big and being faithful in the small?

Dreaming big and being diligent in the small is a life-changing, world-changer combo.

Yet, for years in my twenties I focused solely on the dreaming big aspect and forgot mostly about the diligence it was going to take in the small.

It's hard not to lose hope when the big dream seems 500 miles away. When all you see is highway in front of you, into the horizon, seemingly unending.

When it seems like all your friends are already at their destination and documenting every glorious second of it on social media.

It's hard to chip away. It's hard to plant more seeds. Yet, it's been my experience that God was doing big things in me within the small moments filled with small details.

Without the small, there is no big. It's like filling up a well with buckets of water. People will see the water pouring over only after you've emptied thousands of buckets into it. And man, how strong and determined you'll be from all those buckets you've carried.

Most of our perceived successes and failures don't come down to our own amazing abilities or lack thereof. It comes down to timing.

That's it.

Success or failure really is just about the right or wrong time. And if you're able to persevere and stay faithful to make it to the right time.

At the *proper time* things will blossom, if you do not give up watering the ground. That little sprout might be a day away from bursting through the ground, but you'll never know if you walk away from it too soon.

43

How do I keep my wick from being doused with gasoline and burned at both ends?

The last few months, no matter how much I accomplish or how much progress I make, it never feels like enough.

There's always another . . .

email to send

PAGE TO WRITE

call to make

WEBSITE TO REVIEW

☐ BOX to CHECK

There

IS

always

MORE!

When you're chasing a dream, your legs never stop moving.

When you're building a platform, there's always another brick you need to lay down.

But when is enough, enough?

When you're putting yourself out there, it's hard to know when to take a break from the storefront window.

How do you keep your wick from being doused with gasoline and then burned at both ends?

THE ANSWER

I got the answer while sitting at a conference. Now typically at conferences I have the propensity to become a bursting anxiety-ball, letting other people's amazing stories tempt me to feel terrible about my own.

So at this particular conference as we were led through a group exercise before a session began and I knew I could use the help.

We closed our eyes and were asked to visualize ourselves following a trusted guide up a mountain trail. As I saw myself hiking up, I could feel the weight of the anxiety I was carrying. The guide then led us up to a cabin and as he invited us to step through the door, we were told that the cabin was our heart. In the cabin I opened a door that I'd been refusing to go in for far too long and the guide quietly followed behind me. I felt a sense of peace as I entered the room, then I turned and looked at the guide and he said three words that hit me like a peace bomb:

You Are Enough.

That was it.

And standing in the cabin staring at the guide's face, I began to cry. The guide stared at me, face grizzled and worn from years on the trails, and he let his tears fall with mine.

You are enough washed over me like warm rain. I felt like God was telling me that He didn't care as much about my accomplishments, or lack thereof, as He cared about me. No matter how lacking I felt, He wanted to fill every inch of me with His completeness.

So much of my value was coming from the ebb and flow of success, so I kept getting tossed around by each new wave. **Accomplishing less or more will never be able to sustain me.**

And maybe today you need to hear this as well.

Your identity is not just one thing. You are not just one outcome. There's not one noun that describes you. You're not one job title. You are not defined by one relationship. Your identity should not be tied to one thing like a balloon ready to float away the moment one string is cut.

You are more than the visible outcome of your work.

And the outcome of your work might be more than what is currently visible.

Do good work. Put your dream out there. Do your best to help others.

Then, let it go. Your dream can't fly if your identity and self-worth are clinging on to the back of it.

No matter your success or failure.

No matter your job security or insecurity.

No matter your relationship status.

No matter the names people have tried to define you by.

No matter your shame or your secrets.

No matter what you've done or what is left to do.

No.matter.what. You are enough even when you feel like you haven't done enough.

Chase your dreams. Don't let your dreams chase you.

Do I have anyone on my "Dream Team"?

There might be nothing more powerful and important to achieving a dream than the people you have walking alongside you on the path.

That's why I think everyone needs a Dream Team—a 3–5 person tight-knit group of individuals who have all agreed to keep each other accountable, motivated, and who will support you as you support them.

Write down 3–5 names you'd like to be on your dream team and invite them all out to lunch together or if you live far apart, jump on Google Hangout (or whatever better technology is around when you're reading this book!). Ask if they'd like to intentionally meet at least once a month and support each other in pursuing your dreams, sharing ideas, and encouraging each other.

Nothing is more powerful in pursuing your purpose than the group of people you're pursuing it next to. For example, like the group of writers and professors who called themselves the "Inklings" and met together weekly in an English pub to read aloud, discuss together what they were working on, and give each other feedback.

One of the Inkling's members being J. R. R. Tolkien. Another being C. S. Lewis.

1.

2.

3.

4.

5.

Do I have any glaring Critics, Cynics, or "Reality Checkers" in my life that are doing their best to hold me back?

"REALITY CHECKERS ARE EVERYWHERE AND THEY LOVE DISHING OUT DOSES OF REALITY LIKE THEY'RE A DOCTOR AND THIS IS THE PRESCRIPTION YOU NEED. YOU KNOW THE KIND. WHERE YOU SHARE WITH THEM YOUR EVEREST-SIZED DREAM AND BEFORE YOU CAN EVEN FINISH THEY RATTLE OFF THE SEVEN REASONS YOUR DREAM WON'T WORK. THEY LATHER YOU IN THEIR OWN FEAR AND INSECURITIES, AND CALL IT SOUND ADVICE."

– 101 Secrets For Your Twenties

Critics, Cynics, and Reality Checkers don't really want to see your dreams happen. They might say they do, and then in the same breath they are meticulously tearing apart every aspect of your dream until there's nothing left to touch.

Reality Checkers are especially tricky, because they lather you in their own fear and insecurities and call it sound advice.

Obviously we all need wise, secure people speaking truth into our lives. Yet, letting an extremely insecure person speak into your dreams is as insane as letting a five-year-old tell you how to drive your car. Having discernment about who you take life advice from is sometimes more important than the advice itself.

How can you start limiting the impact critics, cynics, and reality checkers have on your thoughts and forward movement? Write down a few of the main critics, cynics, and reality checkers in your life and then strategies on how you limit their effect and influence on you. Or how do you harness their negativity and turn it into a healthy fuel to rocket-fire you further?

• Critics (love giving constant "feedback," and nothing is ever good enough):

• Cynics (negative people):

• Reality Checkers (love dosing you with "reality," often heard saying *"I'm just trying to be realistic here…"*):

How do I stop "infotainment" from slapping me in the face every five seconds and taking my lunch money?

In the past, finding and acquiring information was a needed skill set to succeed.

The real skillset now is not finding the info, but extrapolating what info you need and what info is good. The skillset is knowing what is pure infotainment and should be avoided. And knowing what is needed info that should be digested and harnessed.

Like a scientist running an experiment, the data doesn't do much good if you don't have control groups that you are comparing the new data to.

So in your life, what are some "control groups" that you can bring the sheer slew of information to?

1. MENTORS, TEACHERS, WRITERS, AND WISE FRIENDS

I definitely have a list of people in my life I turn to for help to make sense of information. Without their expertise and wisdom, I'd be trying to sort through information myself, which would be a grand experiment in how to be overwhelmed and fail miserably. We need a collection of wise people we can turn to for guidance.

2. THE BIBLE

It's the bestselling book of all time for a reason. So much of today's information feels stuffed full of fear, alarms, warnings, contradictions, and infotainment. Taking this swell of info and filtering it through the Bible is an amazing way to stay grounded amidst the info-explosions.

3. OTHER WISE BOOKS AND INFLUENTIAL THINKERS

Instead of seeing what everyone and their mom is saying about something, see what the best thinkers in the world, who have continually built credibility and trust, are saying.

4. YOUR GUT, YOUR CONSCIENCE, YOUR INTUITION

How does the information feel to you? Does it feel on point? Or does it feel like a jagged point that is not sitting well? Sure, we all need to be willing to take in information that on the surface might be something we disagree with, but we do need to trust our instincts and gut feeling when it comes to how we move forward with that information.

IN EVERY GREAT STORY
THE HERO ALWAYS
EXPERIENCES AN
"ALL IS LOST"
MOMENT

BEFORE
THE DRAMATIC RISE.

PAUL
ANGONE

*101 QUESTIONS
YOU NEED TO ASK
IN YOUR TWENTIES*

#101Q

47

Do your actions back up your ambitions? Does your behavior back up your words?

Gary Vaynerchuck asked this question in a recent blog article on his website, and it really convicted me.

If you don't know Gary's story and message, you should. He felt like a failure most of his adolescence as a D/F student. Then at 30 years old, realizing he was not where he wanted to be in life, he started his audacious dream of Wine TV on YouTube, making five videos a week tasting wine. Yet, for a year and a half, he received nothing but 50–75 views a video.

Flash forward ten years and he's now a mega-bestselling author, social media influencer, and CEO of the fastest growing creative agency averaging $150 million in revenue.

How did he get from a struggling dream to a powerhouse company?

Doggedness. Consistent, steady, hard work. He completely owned his Signature Sauce of being Gary Vee and did not listen to all the critics and cynics who said he would never succeed by being himself. **People kept telling him he needed to tone it down while Gary just kept letting those words rev him up.**

He never stopped asking himself that question above—*do my actions back up my ambitions?*

We can talk all we want about doing big things, yet Gary Vaynerchuck is a reminder that your actions must be the backbone of your ambitions.

Comfort and challenge don't play nice together at the same table. *Am I looking for a challenging job or a comfortable one?*

Exponential growth should be the goal of your twenties.

Not just a paycheck. Not just a promotion. But a heightened growth in your skill sets, in your character, and in your learning experiences.

In our twenties and thirties, we shouldn't focus so much on upgrading our material possessions. No, we should be focused on **upskilling** our talents and abilities.

Your work should be challenging you. And you should be engaged in your work to challenge it. To explore ways to do it well and do it better.

"THE MOST DANGEROUS JOB YOU CAN HAVE IN YOUR 20S IS A COMFORTABLE ONE."

— *101 Secrets For Your Twenties*

Your job should be hard. Don't land on easy.

Comfort and challenge don't sit well at the same table.

Don't upscale too quickly. No, upskill instead.

49

It's a lot easier to do something successful once than it is to sustain it. So the question is—why are one-hit wonders, one-hit wonders?

Why do some people reach success and sustain it, while others hit success and then it hits them back with a fury?

Not all success is the same. And not all success is sustainable. Some fall into success and some work to build it from the ground up.

Sometimes the worst thing that can happen to someone is to achieve the exact success they hoped for too quickly.

It's a lot easier to do something successful once than it is to sustain it.

Two examples I'm thinking of as I write this:

1. I just watched the documentary on Amy Winehouse—the pop jazz singer who tragically died of alcohol poisoning and other various addictions at twenty-seven years old. It's a hard documentary to watch in many ways as the success she gained became her downfall, something she couldn't, or didn't want to escape from to get healthy. Her hit song was about refusing to go to rehab, when going to rehab is what she absolutely needed most. Success doesn't diminish your existing struggles and insecurities; it throws gasoline on them.

2. I enjoy reading about Nate Reuss, the lead singer of Fun, a band that hit stratospheric success with their song "We Are Young." They won a Grammy for it 2013 and they also won a Grammy for Best New Artist. Yet, Nate must have laughed at the grand irony of it all. He won "best new artist" after struggling in the music industry for years, even having a fairly successful band called The Format from 2002–2008.

Nate achieved success, then had it all fall apart, then in an elevator cornered a producer who wouldn't take a meeting with him and sang him the chorus to "We Are Young," which he'd just come up with and hadn't even shared with his band. Next thing you know, they're winning best new artist when they were anything but new. Nate has had many successful solo songs since "We Are Young" and Fun's guitar player Jack Antonoff is now the lead singer for a popular band called The Bleachers. Their success faded, went on life support, then was revived stronger and with more purpose.

So if success feels like a labor of love right now, maybe it's because you're building a strong foundation for it. Maybe you're going through the ringer a little right now to save you from going through a dumpster fire later.

50 (ADULT)

Am I bathing in disappointment like a cat taking a nap in its own litter box?

If you're alive and reading this right now, there's a good chance you have something very real to be disappointed about.

A lousy job. Relationship problems. Sickness. Politics. Or life in general is going nothing like you planned. I get it.

We can't avoid disappointment. But when it comes your way, will you crush the disappointment or let it crush you? Will we continually bathe in it or wash it off and keep moving forward? Well, if you've ever smelled a choice litter box before, you know that's probably not the fragrant musk you want to walk into a room with.

So how do we hose off those big disappointments in our lives? Here are some ideas:

1. THINK ABOUT THE PAST DISAPPOINTMENTS IN YOUR LIFE.

I can almost hear you now—

"Great Paul, I'm feeling terrible about my life and now you want me to start thinking about some of my biggest disappointments. Wonderful.

Why don't you just tell me to eat raw chicken and then jump up and down?"

While I don't recommend eating raw chicken (although it would probably put your current disappointments in a different light), I do recommend thinking back to some of your past disappointments. And then think back to how things somehow worked out afterward, and maybe even for the better. Sure, not all disappointments have a clear, visible silver lining, but when I sit back and think about them, usually I'm surprised by how many that do.

Typically when we think our life as we know it is over, our life keeps going.

For example, I remember a girl breaking up with me and feeling disappointed about it. Okay that's an understatement. I felt like she had done the Texas two-step on my heart and then had a horse sit on it. I wasn't disappointed. I was crushed.

Then my good friend Josh gave me this wise advice—

"If you thought this girl was great and yet it wasn't meant to be, think about how amazing the woman you are going to marry is going to be."

And now ten years of marriage and three kids later, what my friend told me was a million times more true than he could've ever known.

Sometimes what we see as a disappointment now is merely a blessing to be discovered later. **You never know how a "disappointment" will look in retrospect.**

2. RELAX AND HAVE FAITH

The more I try to have everything work out exactly how I plan, in exactly my timing, the more disappointed I'm going to be. I know this. Yet, I still try to hold tight to all the details of my day.

The more adaptable I am, the more faith I have that God is working things out better than I ever could, even if I can't see it at the moment, the more peace I have.

It's not a blind faith, it's a faith seeing with eyes wide open how many times God has come through for me.

If we're only looking at what we can see, we will miss everything else that is going on under the surface.

3. BE WILLING TO BE ADAPTABLE

Sometimes the best plan you can make is to plan to continually make new plans.

It's hard to be too disappointed in life if you're willing to adapt your plans when they don't go exactly as planned.

If you let each failed plan and unmet expectation overwhelm you with disappointment, you won't be able to move forward with much in life.

It's only a dead end if you let it stop you. Or you can climb the wall in front of you and get a better view.

Some of my greatest disappointments have led to my biggest achievements. Because they forced me to find a different, better way. I was disappointed mainly because I wanted grand success with minimal effort. Disappointment was birthed more out of my own laziness and ego than anything else.

It's okay to be disappointed. But don't bathe in it. Hose it off, keep the faith, and keep moving forward.

Do I create or do I complain more?

Did you know that complaining actually rewires your brain?

Same with thinking optimistically and looking for new things to create.

Various studies and scientists have shown that your brain is constantly rewiring itself, and the more you, let's say, complain about how terrible work is, the more those synapses and neurons that formed those negative thoughts come closer to each other so that you can have that same thought easier the next time.

The same thing happens in positive, optimistic thoughts. The more you think them, the more common it will be for you to think them again.

As Jeffrey Schwartz, research psychiatrist at UCLA School of Medicine, writes about in his book *You Are Not Your Brain*, repeated thinking patterns literally create ruts in your brain that become hard to escape from.

Yes, every single day presents all of us with a litany of things to complain about. It also presents us with a litany of things to be thankful for.

We can complain more or we can create.

We can consume more or we can create.

We can criticize more or we can create.

We can be reactive to the economy's ebbs and flows or we can be proactive in finding needs and meeting them.

Opportunities for twentysomethings and thirtysomethings haven't disappeared; it just takes a little more *imagination* and *hutzpah* to uncover them.

We can't sit around and wait for the doors to open; we have to keep pounding on them until one swings wide open.

The more you complain, the harder it will be to stop.

The more you create, the easier it will be for you to create again the next day.

Create more. Complain less. Repeat.

How do I grab my fear by the ears and snarl at it?

"Go put this bridle on that horse," my boss said to me. *"And don't touch his ears this time."*

Here are some facts that led up to this statement:

- I was working as a wrangler at the guest ranch in the Rocky Mountains of Colorado.

- I started working there, somewhat inexperienced with horses (I was mainly hired for my rugged good looks—well, that and possibly because I lied a tad on my application), so I was learning on the fly every day. Sometimes very afraid.

- Putting a bridle on a horse consists of typically putting a metal bit into a horse's mouth, and then sliding the leather headgear over the horse's ears and latching it together.

- The horse I was supposed to put a bridle on had just created ten minutes of terrifying anarchy. He ripped an 8-foot, fifty-pound wood rail from a fence and swung it around on a rope like it was a piece of licorice, almost hitting other horses and people in the process, just because another wrangler had touched his ears while trying to put his bridle on.

- My boss, Harold, was one tough cowboy who rode the craziest mules we had on the ranch, all with a handlebar mustache to back it up. When Harold told you to do something, you didn't argue with him.

As I grabbed that bridle and slowly walked toward that horse, what happened next taught me an important lesson about fear.

HOW TO BEAT FEAR

I was terrified as I walked up to that horse, but there was no way I could back out of putting a bridle on. So I slowly walked up to the horse I would've rather just shipped to Montana. Quickly did what my boss had just taught me. And got the bridle on with no problem.

I then walked away a little taller, prouder, and less afraid to do it the next time.

Harold, a man I respected very much, had a leadership style I could sum up like this:

If you're afraid, do it anyway.

It never mattered to Harold who had the most experience or who was the best on paper for a certain task. If you were there, you did the job. For the rest of the summer it was a crash course in learning—

You ease fear by doing it afraid. Then the next time, the fear is a little less frightening.

GET ON AND GET GOING!

As a generation, we've become paralyzed by overanalyzing.

With so much information at our fingertips, we want to research and remove all risk of embarrassment before we'll even put our toe in the water.

When sometimes the best way to learn how to swim is by being thrown in the deep end naked and blindfolded.

Doing something big is scary. Not doing something big because you're afraid is even scarier!

If there's something you know you need to do, but have been too nervous to take that first step, do it right now.

Don't wait for it to feel right. Do it. Then feel right about it after it's done.

If you're scared to speak in public, join a Toastmasters and give a talk.

If you're scared to network, email five people right now you'd like to meet with and compliment them.

Walk into the office you want to be hired at and see if the hiring manager is available.

Go up to the girl you've been texting with and ask her out on a date. In person. With your voice.

Volunteer to head up that big project at work even if you feel it's overwhelming.

Do it. Then figure out how to get it done.

You learn the most by doing the things that you fear you're the least capable of doing.

Move forward in spite of the fear, and then the next time it will be a little less frightening.

53

Am I going through my day mindful or mindless?

In today's world that is constantly warring for our attention and focus, there might be no greater skill to actively cultivate and activate than intentional mindfulness.

The way I see mindfulness is basically being intentional thinkers. It's being aware of what's going on inside and around you. Mindfulness is paying attention to what the details of your day are whispering to you instead of what the world is shouting.

It's going to be hard to answer many of these questions in this book, it's going to be impossible to gain clarity and direction for your life, if you're not bringing intentional thinking and reflection to the process.

We get so wrapped up in the big questions that we forget about the amazing things we are experiencing every day in the small.

We are given gifts of clarity, vision, and calling that go far beyond a self-assessment exam.

Yet, we can't be too busy, too cynical, or too distracted to take notice.

So how do we tangibly and strategically practice mindfulness? Being mindful can feel a little vague and ambiguous, so to help us all practice mindfulness, here are four different mindset models I've created—Writer, Investigator, Entrepreneur, and Monk.

Four Mindset Models . . .

54

How do I practice having a Writer Mindset today?

Some of the best writing I do is when I'm not writing at all! Some of my most insightful writing happens when I'm doing the dishes, taking a shower, playing with my kids, or just driving my car. It's in these day-to-day moments when I'm hit with insight because my mind is actively working on describing an idea or defining a problem. My mind is still writing even if my hands have stopped. Then I've learned to make sure I jot down the thought or insight right away because no matter how important I think the insight is at the moment, I'll still forget it if I don't write it down.

For 1–2 days, try to intentionally focus on going through your day like a writer. Focus on intentionally writing down observations, thoughts, realizations, and "aha" moments that come to you throughout the day. It doesn't matter if you think it's silly or monumental, write it down or record it on your phone.

Keep a running list of these thoughts, and then after 1–2 days, go back to your list and see what stands out as meaningful or important.

How do I practice having an Investigator Mindset today?

I love watching the BBC show *Sherlock*. How he pieces together seemingly random patterns and clues that aren't random at all to solve the case in front of him.

The Investigator Mindset is a great extension of the Writer Mindset because it's finding connections within your observations. It's finding things that are connected to gain strategy on how to best solve different problems or questions in your life.

For 1–2 days, intentionally practice the Investigator Mindset by focusing on patterns, habits, and events that are interconnected. What times in your last 1–2 days did you feel most anxious? Are there any patterns you're noticing? What times in your last 1–2 days did you feel most alive and full of energy? Any patterns? Write these down. Come to your day like an Investigator, and see what you discover. If you're feeling depressed or anxious that nothing in life is going as planned, looking for connections between seemingly disconnected things can help you find meaning in the mundane.

56

How do I practice having an Entrepreneurial Mindset today?

The biggest difference between entrepreneurs and everyone else is that entrepreneurs see problems and obstacles as opportunities. Entrepreneurs see a problem and get excited about it because they want to help create the solution.

If there weren't any problems, there wouldn't be any businesses. Every business exists to solve a problem.

For the next 1–2 days, instead of feeling crushed by the challenges and problems that come your way, what opportunities and possibilities can you envision being birthed out of these problems? Focus on seeing challenges and problems as possibilities and opportunities.

For everything that frustrates you the next two days, write down a possible solution to ease that frustration.

Again, purposeful work isn't created through a lack of struggle; purposeful work is honed and defined in the midst of it.

57

How do I practice having a Monk Mindset today?

Thomas Merton wrote, "Music is pleasing not only because of the sound but because of the silence that is in it: without the alternation of sound and silence there would be no rhythm."

For a couple years in my twenties, I felt like a complete mess. Everything inside me felt a whipped mix of angst, frustration, and confusion. Unease and unrest were my constant companions.

It was during this season that the book *No Man Is an Island* by Thomas Merton became a calming and rooted force in my life. Merton was a Trappist monk for twenty-seven years. His books contain so much depth and life from a man who spent a majority of his life in silence and solitude, observing the world, his faith, and his surroundings with a radical, profound simplicity of the complex.

When my world feels like a roller coaster dangerously close to careening off the tracks, it's crucial that I practice Monk Mindfulness. For me, one tangible way I do that is by going on hikes and getting out in nature. I walk. I pray. I listen to the small sounds around me. There might be no greater calming force in my life than sun, silence, and sitting on a rock.

We need to listen to those moments when the Designer reveals to you His design.

If you're freaked out and anxious about the future, ground yourself in the present.

Literally, right now, read this next paragraph and then put the book down, get to a quiet place, close your eyes, and just be still.

Pay attention to your senses right now. What noises are you hearing? What smells? What are your fingers touching? Paying attention to your senses forces you to be in the now. When you're feeling anxious throughout the day, pause, and do this exercise. It's really hard to feel anxious about the future and uncertainties of life when you're listening, touching, and tasting the "right now" that you're living in.

For 1–2 days, intentionally practice the Monk Mindset Model. Really focus on limiting distractions. Drive in your car or ride on the subway without listening to music. Check your phone and social media less, or if you want to really go crazy, not at all. Go on a hike, walk, or just get in nature. Spend time in prayer or meditation. Not just talking to God, but listening to Him as well. Take a journal with you and write down your thoughts or feelings.

What meaningful words and thoughts are you discovering?

FAILURE DOESN'T RUIN YOUR STORY.

FAILURE HELPS YOU WRITE IT.

PAUL ANGONE | *101 QUESTIONS YOU NEED TO ASK IN YOUR TWENTIES* | #101Q

58 ◆

Am I recognizing the "not-so-chance" encounters in my life?

Every day we're given the gift of what I call "not-so-chance" encounters. Think back to some of your most meaningful relationships in your life and all the details that had to come together at the exact right time for that relationship to happen.

I'm no mathematician, but let's run the numbers here regarding when you meet someone new.

First, the fact you're both alive at the same time in history. Crazy odds!

Second, that you're both in the same spot, at the same time, rather than any other place within the 100+ million miles of earth you could've been instead. That's wild!

Third, all the events and details that led up to bringing you to that specific place—spilling coffee on your shirt before going out that door that led you to go back in, change clothes, thus setting you back five minutes and thirty-seven seconds, going to a coffee shop for a refill and dropping a quarter in line next to someone who just dropped their spoon, and a conversation starts. That's a wild string of events that you could've never planned and orchestrated yourself that brought you in direct contact with someone.

Fourth, that more often than not, you find that you have some crazy connection or mutual experience that creates a space of understanding that strikes you as a "small world" coincidence.

I mean there's probably better odds of dropping a pebble into a small rowboat in the ocean from 30,000 feet up from outside your plane window than there is of you sitting next to that person on that plane!

Yet, all too often we try our best to pretend the person next to us on the plane doesn't exist. Or the person we met at the party was just an insignificant coincidence. Or we just try to avoid strangers altogether because we're too busy. I am far too guilty of this.

Yet, it's these "not-so-chance" encounters that oftentimes open more doors of opportunity for you than any A in History class or job search site will ever do. There's even the sociological theory about the power of "loose ties"—these "random" acquaintances that end up being the exact person you needed to meet at the exact time to take you to the exact place you were dreaming of.

I recently had a very glaring "not-so-chance" encounter when I was having coffee in Colorado with an acquaintance that I hadn't spoken to in twenty years. He told me a story about a book he was working on and a crazy "not-so-chance" encounter he had meeting a well-connected New York literary agent who was now helping him find a publisher.

Thirty minutes later after hearing about his amazing story of meeting this New York agent, a man walked past our table and my friend looked at him and his face went into shock. It was the same exact New York agent that he just told me the story about! And my friend didn't even know he was in Colorado for the day.

Since then I've had three conversations with the agent about representing me. Obviously, this "not-so-chance" encounter is a glaring one since my friend just told me a story about him, he lives in another state, and is an agent for book authors, and I happen to be one!

However, there are so many other "not-so-chance" encounters that happen that are less obvious, but even more important.

Are you noticing the new "not-so-chance" encounters in your life? And are you appreciating and valuing the "not-so-chance" relationships you already have that maybe you've been taking for granted?

Because that stranger sitting next to you right now is something beyond mundane, it's miraculous.

Am I putting myself in places where I can meet people and start "relationshipping" more?

I believe going to conferences in your twenties and thirties is one of the most strategic ways to meet new people in a career field you're interested in.

Yet, I believe you should go to conferences and attend very little (if any) of the actual conference sessions.

Go to the conference, but don't really go to the conference. Sounds crazy? It is!

The real importance of a conference is the people you meet, not the info you receive. Not only in meeting the conference speakers and influencers there, but also in connecting with the loneliest people at the conference who are desperately looking to make connections—the vendors trying to sell you stuff that most people avoid.

If you've been at a conference, most likely you've had to walk through the **Hall of Awkward**, where rows of vendors from various companies are there to connect with people. Yet, most people scurry through the Hall of Awkward as fast as possible and avoid these vendors like they have a contagious disease.

Big mistake.

At those tables are insider connections to a company that you'd never have an opportunity to have a conversation with otherwise. Plus, these vendors are typically bored, feeling awkward themselves because everyone is awkwardly avoiding them, and they want to talk to someone. Anyone. *Please Lord, just help me pass the time.*

So if you're a kind, gracious person who sparks a good conversation, you will be like a beacon of hope in their boring day.

I was once a college recruiter who spent two months manning tables at college fairs where I'd try to have conversations with high-school students about my college. I can't even begin to tell you how much I appreciated those brave students who would come up, shake my hand, look me in the eyes, and have a good conversation with me, even if they weren't that interested in my school.

Some of those students later on would apply to the college and weren't exactly slam dunks on paper to be admitted with their GPA and test scores. However, I strongly made their case to the dean of admissions and persuaded her to admit many of them because of the impression they made on me. They became more than a piece of paper, they were a person who I wanted to see succeed.

So I encourage everyone to go to conferences and do what I call the "awkward wander." No real agenda. No real plan. Just kind of awkwardly wander around and meet people.

I can point to many of the biggest breakthroughs of my career happening at a conference because I did the awkward wander. Thankfully, I excel at awkward.

At one conference a sign at a vendor table caught my eye so I went to talk to the sales rep there. Turns out she worked for the publisher that years before had turned me down three separate times for my book *All Groan Up*. No one else was around and looking to talk, so we chatted for about twenty minutes about all kinds of different things. Toward the end of the conversation, I told her about my passion for helping twentysomethings and the writing I was doing, and her eyes lit up—"Wow, I think the VP of marketing would love to meet you. He shares the same passion."

That one conversation from doing my awkward wander led to a book deal with the publisher that had turned me down three times before when I had a literary agent and had looked way more official.

The power of a quality connection with a real person goes far beyond what any well-crafted book proposal, resume, or GPA could ever do for you.

What conference can you go to? Research some today. Pick one. And start awkwardly wandering around and relationshipping.

60

What am I going to regret NOT doing?

I had a reader named Jason reach out to me through Twitter after reading *101 Secrets For Your Twenties,* and this was the question he asked me—what did I regret *not* doing sooner in life? A great question!

Oftentimes we talk about the things we regret doing, but it's the regret of things never attempted that can sometimes be the heaviest weight to carry later in life.

My answer?

Not taking more big risks.

Not daredevil type risks, but risks to go after something bigger, something that felt unreachable and uncomfortable. Seeking out risks instead of avoiding them. Letting the fear of embarrassment hold me back.

It's like the old saying goes—you never receive because you never ask. Well, maybe you don't have because you don't risk. The biggest risk you can take in your twenties and thirties is not taking any risks at all.

61

Who will you not be able to help if you give up now?

You can't give up.

On your dream, on your passion, on this vision for your life that extends farther and further than your current reality.

You can't pull an Elsa and just *let it go*—shooting shards of ice at anyone who brings up those dreams you used to talk about.

No matter how distant your dreams feel right now. No matter how hard the path. No matter how unrealistic it feels right now.

You can't give up.

Here's why.

Who will you not be able to help if you give up now?

There are people out there. You might not even know they exist. And they need you. They need your voice, creativity, talent, insight, encouragement.

And if you quit now, you won't be there when they need you the most.

Your moment is waiting for you. If you stop looking, how will you ever find it?

I know, because a few years ago I was a week away from quitting.

The dream was too much work, too painful, and all the writing on the wall was smacking me in the face and screaming at me to stop this silly dream.

And yet, something told me to hold on.

All the facts were telling me that quitting was the smart, reasonable choice. Yet, deep in my spirit I knew that the ripples of quitting now were going to extend further than I could see. I was writing to give truth, hope, and hilarity to others, and if I stopped putting words down, no matter if people were reading it or not, then all the ripples would be nonexistent.

QUITTING CREATES THE DE-RIPPLE EFFECT.

Yes, you can't control the outcome of your dream. And as I mentioned earlier in the book, you have to let your expectations go of how exactly you thought your dream should end up.

Yet, the moment when you feel like you absolutely can't go any further is about three steps before you start to really see the progress you've been making all along.

I had a week left before I completely quit my dream, and that's when I posted an article called "21 Secrets for Your 20s" that went viral and finally became that tipping point that I so desperately needed.

Now years later, the emails and stories I receive from people all over the world who have been touched by something I've written completely astounds and amazes me every time. It's all much bigger than me. Much larger than even the dreams I used to have that once felt so big and unrealistic.

You see, you can't quit. You just can't. If you've been wavering back and forth—consider this your sign to keep going.

The world needs your passion, dreams, vision, and values. The world needs your story.

Someone out there right now needs your dream, and neither of you know it.

Don't give up. Don't stop asking yourself these hard questions.

Keep chipping away. It might be 11:59 p.m. for you right now. You never know what last stroke might lead to your breakthrough.

62

How do I find my "77% sure" and just move forward?

For years in my twenties, I think much of my angst came because I was subconsciously searching for that perfect path to my future that didn't exist.

The search for perfect is the perfect way to be perfectly miserable.

There is no perfect job. No perfect partner. No perfect friend. No perfect time. No perfect family. No perfect church. No perfect neighborhood. No perfect answer. No perfect path.

You'll never have enough information. Or the perfectly uninhibited view.

The only thing you're going to find on your search for perfection is a bunch of imperfections to be depressed about. As I wrote in *101 Secrets For Your Twenties*, "Are you freaked out that you have no idea what you're doing? Perfect! So is everyone else."

Life is about navigating the imperfect instead of trying to grab hold of a perfect illusion. We will never have all the information we need.

Glorious, uncomfortable ambiguity. When the smartest thing you can do is find your "77% sure" and move forward. When you feel that nudge in a direction, follow it. See where it leads. You'll only know what's around the corner if you walk up to it and peer around.

63

What are my Top 5 soul values?

I'd describe soul values as beliefs that are fundamental to how you are wired, guiding your actions, thoughts, plans, and purpose on this earth.

One of my mentors, Ray Rood, was the first person who challenged me to write down my top values in order from most important on down through a process he created called "Strategic Futuring." Ranking my top values was an incredibly difficult and helpful process. We all think we know our values, and yet I realized then that I'd never really sat down to define them.

We all have values that direct us and help us make decisions—the problem is most of us have never articulated what those values are. We think we know our top values, yet sitting down and articulating exactly what they are can be incredibly difficult.

The purpose of your soul values is really to be a guiding force in your life. When you're at a crossroads, when you're trying to make decisions about your future, when you're working through relationship issues or working on a six month life plan—all these situations can be guided by soul values. For most of my twenties, I felt like a failure because I wasn't paying attention to my soul values, so instead I kept sabotaging myself. I was trying to make some other person's definition of success my own.

If you're feeling anxious or frustrated about a job you're working in, a relationship you're involved with, or a decision you're trying to make, I've often found that the anxiety is actually the by-product of an important soul value of yours that is in conflict.

Our soul values can, and will, even trump our strengths.

Take me for example, one of my strengths is communication so I always thought I should be doing a sales job. Yet often times I'd find myself miserable, and doing a lousy job, in sales positions. I'd leave work feeling like a complete failure because one of the few strengths I thought I had was getting me nowhere. I'd drive home wondering if I was just gifted with a complete lack of gifts.

But then it hit me. I wasn't doing a terrible job in my sales position because of my strength or weakness in communication. I was doing a lousy job because the sales position was contradicting one of my highest soul values—authenticity. I struggle being in a job, friendship, situations, etc., where I feel like I have to pretend to be someone else. It makes me feel anxious and that I'm lying to everyone, including myself.

In that sales position, I didn't believe in what I was selling, so my soul value for authenticity was trumping my strength in communication and actually turning it into a weakness.

So it's crucial that we take the time to think about what values truly guide our decisions and actions. Literally rank them in order from top to bottom, with your number one value trumping all. Think back to your major triumphs and tragedies you wrote about earlier in this book and what soul values you can see embedded in those experiences.

Again this exercise is something to keep coming back to, so don't feel like this is set in stone.

1.

2.

3.

4.

5.

Is there a soul value I have that I feel like I'm not currently living by? Why? What can I do about it?

Can you spot within your soul values any that are in conflict right now in your life and work? If so, what can you do to change that?

I wouldn't change your soul value. I'd try to change the circumstance, person, or thing trying to destroy it.

Yet, sometimes we need to be flexible and adaptable in our soul values. Sometimes we need to change our expectations of how living by that soul value looks and feels on a day-to-day basis. For example, maybe you have a value of adventure, yet can you always be running around like Indiana Jones, saving 16th-century Spanish artifacts from aliens? Well, unless Steven Spielberg is your uncle, probably not.

Sometimes we need to change our situation to align with our

values. Other times we need to tweak our expectations of that value to thrive in a situation.

If this sounds less than straightforward, it is. The beauty and struggle of "adulting" is in the small day-to-day decisions and bringing as much wisdom to those decisions as possible. Will you always say or do the "right" thing? Probably not. But if you string together more decisions that align with your soul values than not, you might be amazed at where your path takes you.

Who inspires me the most?

If you're having trouble pinning down your soul values, a good way to figure out what values are most important to you is by defining what most impresses you in others.

The person you want to be like the most tells you a lot about who you hope to become.

Think about the 2–3 people you most want to emulate. It could be a historical figure, someone you know personally, someone who you follow closely, or a ravenously handsome author with three kids who writes books for twentysomethings—just to name a few.

What specifically is it about them that draws you to them?
What is it about their story, character, or actions that you respect? Write down the words that come to mind to describe them next to their names below.

1.

2.

3.

66

Do my soul values repel or compel my significant other's soul values?

One of the greatest causes for conflict in marriage is contradicting soul values.

Again, I'd describe soul values as beliefs that are fundamental to how you are wired, guiding your actions, thoughts, plans, and purpose on this earth.

We all have values that direct us and help us make decisions—problem is, most of us have never articulated what those values are.

And if you don't know your values, how can you expect your partner to have a clue?

Not all values are the same, and sometimes you can have two very good people with very good values, but those values can feel at war with each other.

If your core values can't dance together, then you'll keep tripping, falling, and wondering why you can't move together in rhythm.

For example, you could have a high value for responsibility, and the person you're dating could have a high value for risk. Both values are good, but if not articulated and discussed, it could be a point of high conflict if the responsible person likes consistency and persistence, while the risk-taker likes changing things up and going for the impossible.

Too many marriages start (and end) with vague and unidentified core values.

67

Do I like who I am when I'm with my partner?

Are you really being *you* when you're with them?

Or are you constantly trying to hide who you are because they want you to be someone you're not?

Are you fitting and conforming to some abstract idea of what you think they want? Or are you blossoming and flourishing into who you really are?

Which leads to the next question . . .

Does my partner challenge me to be a better, authentic version of myself?

Is your partner trying to force you to become some figment of their unrealistic dating imagination? Or are they challenging you to become a better, authentic you? Not trying to completely change you, but trying to bring the best to the top.

A spouse should be like a gold miner, going under the surface to uncover the invaluable stuff underneath.

Is the person you're dating like a magnet trying to bring the best of you to the surface?

Or are they trying to bury you under a pile of dirt?

**SOMETIMES
THE MOST INSPIRED
THING YOU CAN DO
IS TO KEEP
SHOWING UP**

**WHEN YOU FEEL
COMPLETELY
UNINSPIRED.**

PAUL
ANGONE

*101 QUESTIONS
YOU NEED TO ASK
IN YOUR TWENTIES*

#101Q

We all go through intense communication training for years; it's called childhood. How does my family communicate? How does my partner's family communicate? And are my partner and I communicating about the crazy ways we've learned how to communicate crazily?

It only takes one Thanksgiving dinner of intentionally listening and studying your family to realize that the cranberry cheese log on the table makes more sense sometimes than your family does.

And it's hard to unwire eighteen years of being shown how to talk and listen to others in family situations.

Sure we're not our parents, and we can work to change our communication habits. And this does not mean that if your family didn't exactly model healthy communication that you'll never have healthy relationships. If having a difficult childhood precluded us from getting married or having healthy relationships, there would be about thirteen marriages out there.

However, it is good for all of us to realize that for many of us, our fallback communication plan will be the one our parents laid out for us.

Holidays, especially, are giving you a glimpse into how your partner has been taught and trained on how to communicate. Don't just sit back and eat that holiday ham. Sit up, take notes, because believe me you'll want to feel prepared for the test that comes later.

And this test will come like a train on a dark and stormy night when your car runs out of gas on the tracks! I promise.

Have I tackled my relationship monsters?

We all have insecurities, fears, failures, painful memories, and just all around unattractive stuff we're hiding in the back of our closest.

Like that yearbook from our awkward years, we all have things we hope no one will ever lay eyes on.

However . . .

Just because you want to pretend your monsters don't exist doesn't mean they're just going to magically go away.

And especially in relationships, they have the amazing ability to take all that you hoped remained hidden and put it on stage for a nationally televised interview that your in-laws will be watching and making mental notes on.

Tackle your monsters now. Don't let them crush your relationship later.

As I wrote in *101 Secrets For Your Twenties:* "**Stop looking for the right person and focus on becoming the right person**. Sure that doesn't mean you close your eyes while walking around the grocery store or that you'll ever be a *completely* healthy person ready for a relationship. However, *right attracts right*. And *the* more *right* you are, *the more right* your relationship will be."

I don't think we ever fully get rid of these monsters—we just quiet their roar.

However, the more skeletons you can face in your closet now, the more monsters you can tackle and then throw out the back door, the better off and more prepared you'll be for marriage and parenting.

The more monsters you try to sneak into marriage, the scarier marriage is going to feel for a while.

In our marriage or dating relationship, have we discussed our vision for the future together? What does the story of our marriage look like? (If I'm not dating anyone, but want to, what do I envision a fulfilling, healthy marriage to look like?)

Your marriage is for the rest of your future, so it amazes me when couples don't discuss with each other what they want their future to look like. What does your vision of a healthy marriage and the details of the day together look like?

Do you envision your marriage as this career-crushing power couple doing backstrokes together in your quite robust stock portfolio?

Do you envision your marriage serving the poor together, traveling the world while making it a better place?

Do you envision kids running all around the house? Or do you envision dogs (which you treat like they are kids) instead?

If you envision pushing your Schnoodle around the neighborhood in a stroller instead of a human baby, well, that might be something worth discussing.

Sure, what you want in life will change. But you need to discuss the general direction of where you are going as a couple, and then it will be much easier to make those changes along the way.

If five years into your marriage you start walking your cat around on a leash without any prior notice, well, that might come as a little shock.

If I'm being brutally honest with myself and this dating relationship, do I absolutely trust my partner with my life?

"Do I love this person?" is often the litmus test for whether or not you should be in a relationship.

But I'd argue a more complete and insightful question should be: "do I believe in, and do I believe, the person I'm dating?"

Do I trust this person is a question just as important as do I love them. Maybe it's even more important because it's really going to be hard to sustain a loving marriage if trust is not at the foundation of your love. When you are dating someone, it's easy to be caught up in feelings of love, even when the relationship is unhealthy. Yet, it's really hard to artificially create trust.

As an example of this, I don't think there's a better picture of trust, love, and belief than World War II.

Okay, so admittedly we don't think about war as the epitome of love. However, I'm a WWII junkie, and whenever I read accounts from the soldiers fighting in their foxholes in amazing books like *Citizen Soldier* and *Band of Brothers*, both by historian Stephen Ambrose, I'm always struck by the fact that it was mainly trust and love that carried each soldier through some of the most horrific situations imaginable.

Specifically in *Band of Brothers* about the Easy Company Paratroopers, these men went through excruciating and difficult training together, only to fight for years in excruciating and difficult battles. And the main thing that carried them through some of the most horrific circumstances imaginable was a deep, rooted trust and love for the guy in the foxhole with them. They'd built that trust together in training and literally put their lives in the hands of the guy next to them, believing that he was going to stay the course, that he wasn't going to run or leave his comrade behind.

Their ability to be an effective soldier was built on the bedrock of trust.

I think the same thing can be said about dating and marriage. If trust is not the bedrock, then the whole thing is just waiting to fall apart. If you can't trust, you can't love. If you can't trust, you're going to think the person next to you is going to take off once the fighting gets intense.

If you can't trust this person, then your relationship will be built on fear instead of faith in each other. Your relationship will be this insecure mess of constantly wondering what your partner is *really* doing.

If you can't believe, and believe in, the person you're dating, then your love is built on a crumbling foundation.

Yet, sometimes the trust issue might be more your issue than it is theirs. Maybe your partner has done nothing to break your trust, but because of some of your past "relationship monsters" rearing their ugly heads, your partner can never do anything to prove their trustworthiness. You're constantly trying to catch them breaking your trust even when they are not, and in that obsession, your relationship is breaking.

In this case, you might need to dive deep into the pain and fear that is dissolving trust before it can grow. You might to hang tough in that foxhole and get down to the root of your own stuff, even when your heart is screaming at you to run.

Trust is a tricky business, but if both sides of the relationship are being honest with themselves, and each other, letting vulnerability and humility rule the day more than pride and self-defense, then trust has a better chance of becoming an impenetrable defense.

So in your dating relationship, you must ask yourself this question: Has trust repeatedly been shattered and glued back together? Or, like the *Band of Brothers*, can you absolutely trust that this person in the foxhole with you is going to stay the course and protect you? And you in turn, will protect them? Sometimes that might look like having the courage to ask each other hard questions, and give equally hard answers.

If you're constantly trying to convince yourself that you can trust this person, even though they keep proving otherwise, is that really the foxhole you want to jump into for the rest of your life?

What if you're already married and trust is on life support? How do you begin to forgive, or ask for forgiveness, and start putting the pieces back together? This is an incredibly difficult process to go at alone, so which mentors and counselors can help you in this process? Don't try to revive trust all by yourself.

73

What's my family's story?

It's one thing to test your DNA to see where your family line is from. It's a whole other thing, and I'd argue much more important, to understand *the story* of your family line.

Every family has a story—the good, the bad, and the awkward. It's important that you start identifying and understanding some of the cycles that have been prevalent in your family—even if you don't plan to get married, but especially if you do.

Some of these cycles will be positive traits, characteristics, and legacies that you want to repeat and build upon. Then other cycles might feel like strongholds holding your family back that you might need to work with all your might to break.

For example, I love and cherish my Grandpa Edward Swanson. He passed at ninety-seven years old a few years ago, so I had the opportunity to hear many of his stories and learn about his legacy.

As an extremely hard-working man who grew up on the farm and then worked at rock quarries and in factories, some of the positive traits and characteristics that he stood for that I aim to emulate are his steady, consistent, persevering, hardworking nature, even in extremely tough circumstances. Embedded in his DNA, beyond being Swedish, was this farmer Kansas stock that knew the definition of working hard and providing for a family. That's part of his legacy that I want to pass down to my kids.

Yet, in hearing many of my grandpa's life stories, another characteristic that definitely was prevalent in his life was not taking risks and not standing up for himself because of fear. He had the mentality that his lot was something he could not change, and he worked many years in a factory that was miserable for him because he didn't believe he could achieve anything better for himself. I've seen this trait and its effects down my family line, and it's not a trait I want for my own life or for my children and children's children's lives.

There are aspects of my grandpa's legacy that I want to carry forth for my children, and then there are aspects that I want to break for them.

How about for you (within the context of the main players in your family's story)?

74

Everyone leaves a legacy behind. What will mine be? What are 2-3 legacies that I want to pass down to my family, future family, and/or community?

▲75

What are 2-3 cycles that I want to break and not leave behind for my family?

We all have *those* stories in our family line, yet the biggest problem within a family line is when the same story, with different characters, keeps repeating itself.

Whether it's addictions, affairs, greed, pride, poverty, jealousy, or just the propensity to quit when things get too hard. We all have some negative plotlines passed down to us. Have you seen that play out in your family line?

Now, don't get me wrong, these cycles are not easy to break. Whether the source is genetic, spiritual, mental, or all of the above, it's not like we just snap our fingers and *poof, my family is no longer in poverty or depression.*

Yet, the more ingrained these cycles are in your family history, the more intentional you need to be to break them off of you and your future family legacy. Through prayer, counseling, mentorship, and personally making different decisions in those crossroad moments.

All of this is difficult, yet incredibly freeing. You are not the sins of your father. You have the opportunity to change the course for you and your family line forever.

Break the cycles. Change your trajectory. Do it for you and everyone who will follow.

If we want more well-behaved kids, we need more well-behaved parents. What kind of parent do I want to be?

Whether you're twenty-one-years-old and this question feels as relevant to you as asking what's your highest shuffleboard score. Or you have kids already and fully understand what it's like trying to corral a few baby monkeys while diapering a koala hyped up on cane sugar.

Whether you have kids right now or not, I don't think it's ever too early to ask, think about, and remind ourselves what kind of parent we want to be.

Being a good parent is not an automatic response. Because kids will stretch you like that slime from the dollar store that quickly breaks and becomes fully embedded in your white carpet.

Being a good parent is something that you have to work at while chaos is sometimes sitting directly on your head. Being a good parent requires you to be a good person. It's really hard to be a good parent when you haven't tackled your own monsters yet. Because the little monsters fighting each other on the floor will draw out your big monsters like a steak to a T-Rex.

The healthier you can become, the better parent you'll be.

Am I building my Grown-Up Sandcastle too close to the ocean?

Adulthood is won in the small, daily things.

I know this. Yet, here's how too many days go for me: I stay up too late watching TV. Then I wake up late and groggy. Then I feel rushed and am trying to explode the morning cobwebs in my brain with massive amounts of quickly consumed caffeine. Then the caffeine starts working on overdrive and I begin feeling anxious, my heart screaming, "Hey, I'm not supposed to be beating this fast! What have you done to me?"

Then the rest of the day, I'm doing this dance of eating too much sugar, getting a quick rush, and then feeling bogged down again, drinking more coffee, feeling a slight rush before I smack head first into a wall again, etc., etc.

It's like being on a possessed carnival carousel ride, spinning me around and around with an overwhelming mix of music, mirrors, and nausea.

On the other hand, then I have the nights when I go to bed at a reasonable time and wake up earlier, feeling mostly refreshed. I step outside on my back porch and slowly sip coffee while I pray and let all those morning smells seep into me. Then I step into my day with energy and brain power, and I'm more apt and able to make wiser choices about what I eat and how much coffee I drink.

Your late night and early morning has the power to make or break your entire day. It's like giving yourself a head start in a race, instead of beginning ten feet behind while pulling a wagon filled with old tube TVs playing nothing but the *Brady Bunch*.

Is there a way you can do your late night and morning routine better? Starting every day on the wrong foot, then becoming frustrated that you're not making much progress in life, is like building a sandcastle too close to the ocean. As the tide comes in and out, everything will keep getting washed away. Instead of constantly rebuilding the castle, just move it to a better place.

DOING SOMETHING BIG IS SCARY.
NOT DOING SOMETHING BIG BECAUSE YOU'RE AFRAID

IS EVEN SCARIER!

PAUL ANGONE | *101 QUESTIONS YOU NEED TO ASK IN YOUR TWENTIES* | #101Q

78

Am I seeing
my own life
for the crazy
miracle that
it is?

You are a miracle.

As Dr. Ali Binazir broke down in a Harvard blog:

"So what's the probability of your existing? It's the probability of 2 million people getting together—about the population of San Diego—each to play a game of dice with *trillion-sided dice*. They each roll the dice, and they all come up the exact same number— say, 550,343,279,001."

Alright, why do I bring this up?

First, I know what it's like to struggle with depression, where life feels very grim and hopeless. Depression is really hard to go through and hard to break out of. I've gone through different seasons of my life where I've felt all alone and wondered if God actually cared about me.

So when I see the odds of me being born, it reminds me of the intentionality that brought me here. It reminds me that I'm not some chance mistake. We are "fearfully and wonderfully made" (Psalm 139:14). While this thought and realization is not some magic elixir to heal depression, it's definitely a powerful piece of light when my emotions and thoughts try to pull me into some dark pit.

Second, the way you're wired. The way you think. Your signature sauce, that flavor you bring to the world, is not a mistake either.

Look at the odds of you being here right now—if you don't believe you're here for a reason, well you've got more faith than me. When the world starts shouting at you the opposite. When your thoughts and emotions want to take a headfirst dive down.

Be still and know.

Be still and know that God has been actively engaged in your life since before it began.

79

Am I holding my dreams hostage and demanding that I pay the ransom?

Holding yourself hostage, and then demanding you pay the ransom, doesn't exactly sound like a smart move. Yet, too many of us are doing just that.

What do I mean?

I know in my life, all too often it feels like I have two different people inside of me working toward completely opposite goals.

A constant battle is being fought, yet not on the frontlines. It's a true inside job. We put our defenses up, fortify them, then go back into our tent, and our dreams are being held hostage by us.

What do I mean? How are we actually sabotaging ourselves? And how do we stop it?

1. APATHY

Apathy is a great defense mechanism to always keep you on the defensive. If you never act like you care about anything too much, then you can never be disappointed too much.

Apathy is wrapped in cynicism and tucked inside a big ball of insecurity. It feels cool. It feels protected. It feels like a great way to do nothing while you try to pick apart everyone who is doing something.

Yet, pain, hurt, and frustration can sit right next to you on your bed as you do nothing just the same as if you stepped out of the house and tried. **I'll take the pain of trying and knowing what doesn't work over the pain of never knowing and always wondering.**

2. BUSYNESS

Busyness is a tricky one because you're working, yet you're working at the wrong things. Too many of us escape into a frantic frenzy of movement because we're scared if we stop, we will have to listen to those whispers, asking, "What are you *really* doing?"

Making progress in the wrong direction is like dropping a bowling ball down a well—you're moving fast, but where are you going to end up?

3. DRAMA!

Do you have people in your life with a *Drama!* Addiction?

Where drama leads, follows, and encompasses them wherever they float to next, like this swirling black hole trying to suck you into *Oh My Gosh did you see what they did to me?!*

We must squelch the drama in our lives. We must refuse to take the bait. There are too many real challenges in life to deal with to be swirling around in circles with unnecessary drama.

WE NEED TO STOP SABOTAGING OURSELVES

Can you spot any ways you might be sabotaging yourself right now? Write them down below.

There are enough challenges to face on the outside to be fighting against a mutiny raging within.

During an average day at work, what's my Dread/Tolerate/ Love percentage breakdown?

Let's make a chart. (This will be fun!)

Look at a typical work day. Break down each hour. Emails, meetings, travel, talking with customers, making products—whatever it is that fills your day at work.

Now let's examine your typical day at work through Dread, Tolerate, and Love. Take your hour breakdown and place each item in one of those three categories. Fill in the pie chart and see what's taking up the majority of your day.

Workday DTL Pie Chart

(Dread, Tolerate, Love)

When looking at this completed chart, does it make you nauseated or happy?

Sure, we're not going to love every aspect of our job, but when your work is filled with more love than dread, I think you'll do much better work. Define what you love about your job and then refine your job to do more of what you love.

Now if your current job appears to be taking up permanent residence in the Land of Dread, does that mean you should be looking to leave that job?

Well, maybe. Or maybe not. Before you leave, I'd first encourage you to find that One Thing. Even if your job is filled with 99% Dread, find at least one thing you love and work at growing your skill set there.

Is there a way you can tackle more projects in your "Love" category? Can you pivot your current job responsibilities to start working more in what you love? Maybe this means coming up with a few ideas and meeting with your manager to see if there are possibilities there for slight changes. I think every manager will want to hear you out if you're leading the conversation from a place of wanting to be more productive and effective for the company. If the manager refuses to even talk to you about it or shuts you down, well now you have at least more clarity about your future there.

Can you find someone in your job who is doing more of a role you'd love to do, and start strategically shadowing them and asking them questions so you can learn more about what they're doing? On-the-job shadowing while you're getting paid to do your job is a wonderful thing. Obviously, that means you still need to do your job, but you can learn a ton from your coworkers every day.

For example, my last "8-5" office job was working as a marketing specialist at a university. It was my favorite job, filled with much more love than dread. Yet, that didn't mean I passed up the opportunity to learn from the talented people around me. I worked very closely on a team with a wonderful creative designer and editor. Every day, within our daily scope of work and projects, I was learning from them about design strategies and effective copywriting, growing my skill set and knowledge in both arenas, while also growing my knowledge in marketing strategies from my amazing leaders in the office as well.

The most profound learning you do about finding work you love doesn't come at school; it comes at work.

It's very tempting to run away as fast as possible from a job that is filled with dread. Or as I learned from watching the Mayor of Starbucks that I wrote about in *101 Secrets For Your Twenties*, for years I was focused on finding the right job instead of bringing the right *me* to every job I worked.

Don't worry so much about finding the "right" job.

Be more focused on your job getting the "right" you.

Don't do a lousy job at your lousy job, or more lousy jobs await.

Too many of us want to escape our lousy jobs before we've grown in a skill set that we can leverage into a better opportunity. If you leave your lousy job without learning and growing, chances are your next job won't be much better.

Your twenties are about putting in the work now so that you can really enjoy your work later.

If I do this now, how am I going to feel about this later?

Getting into an argument with your partner, friend, or manager and feeling your temper beginning to blaze at forest fire levels? *How am I going to feel about this later?*

Letting Netflix take control of you and watching four episodes in a row when you said you were only going to watch one? *How am I going to feel about this later?*

Sitting down to do your work, struggling to feel inspired, and yet still plugging away and making good progress. *How am I going to feel about this later?*

We are all given daily crossroads. Where we can take our day into the good place or into the bad. Before you take a step, think about how you're going to feel if you make a good decision and how you're going to feel if you make a bad one.

Emerging into adulthood is thousands of minutes, hours, and days strung together. Those who are crushing "groan up" life, and those who are being crushed by it, are simply making wise or unwise decisions in the very small. The "insignificant" decisions of the day, like what do I eat for lunch, how do I spend these extra fifteen minutes, etc., exponentially add up over time. People who are making progress in their twenties are stringing together one smart decision after another in the daily small.

Each wise choice in the small building something substantial over time.

Make wise decisions in the daily small. It has the power to make or break adulting for you. We can't swerve each day into one rut after another and then wonder why we're not making any progress.

82

What are my 3-5 favorite stories (books, movies, plays, historical accounts, etc.)?

This question might feel like an AP English exercise, but when trying to write your story, it is a powerful exercise to see what stories most resonate with you.

It's not just by chance that you love these stories. When a story speaks to your soul it's because you're experiencing a story that is entering deep into the heart of *your* story. It's going beyond reason and logic, and entering into your deep-rooted desires, experiences, and emotions.

1.

2.

3.

4.

5.

83

Can I spot any themes and similarities in these favorite stories that resonate with my own life story?

The stories you love reveal a lot about the story you want to live. For example, the common thread that runs through my favorite stories—the underdog who perseveres through pain, finds and then thrives from their authentic self, and succeeds at something sane people would never attempt.

Write down below any consistent themes you spot in your stories. Does this give you more clarity about the story you want to live?

Creating something new is a courageous fight against "the way it's always been." What will I create?

What will I create?

It's a question that asks you to fully be *you*. In business, art, writing, relationships, parenting, working a lousy job, cooking—wherever life finds you right at this moment—**your success will hinge on how creative you will allow yourself to be.**

I choose to create. Here is what I stand for. *Will you join me?*

The Creative Manifesto

- To create is to simply step into how I was created to be. If I'm going to truly be someone, I better be comfortable being myself.

- Creating is a courageous fight against "the way it's always been." To bring forth something inside you that's been waiting for its chance to speak.

- To truly do good art is to pay attention. We're living in a masterpiece. To create is to simply take notes.

- To create something new is to hold someone's face and show them what they've walked past countless times before.

- I don't want to just listen to music. I want to hear it. To feel it. To let it seep into my bones like a sponge. I don't want to listen to a thousand songs. I want to truly sing just one.

- It's easy to follow instructions. It's harder, yet more rewarding, to create your own.

- To create is to take the best of who we are and let it find a home within a medium.

- Creating is to infuse our purpose, personality, and potential into the work set before us. To live uncreatively is to mindlessly consume life like it's a tray of packaged cafeteria food.

- The world will be inherited by those who can see it differently than everyone else.

"WHENEVER YOU'RE DOING SOMETHING WORTH DOING, THE LIAR'S GOING TO ATTACK. EVERY. SINGLE. TIME."

— *101 Secrets For Your Twenties*

- I will not let *The Liar* take me out. When I sit down to do my work, he will begin to speak doubt and fear into me. I will spot his lies before they come. He has no authority over me. I don't want to live pretty and put-together. The only way to make something is to first make a mess.

- Creating, at the core, is telling the truth. It's honesty at its rawest form. It's scraping your knuckles. It's licking the teardrop. To create is to present something to the world that you've been 100% present within.

- Creating is not impartial. When you create, you are taking a side. You are making intentional choices. You are taking a stand.

You are committing through form, medium, brush, song, written word. Every choice is creating meaning. Every creative choice is arguing a point without having to argue.

- It's hard to create anything worth creating if you're expecting to be affirmed and applauded in the process of creating it.

- I will not create expecting everyone to understand what I'm creating.

- I will not create for the critics and the cynics.

- Critics love tearing down what you've built. Yet they've never built anything themselves. Taking creative advice from a critic is like asking your hammer how to paint.

- Every innovator was told it's impossible.

- Every artist battled and was baffled.

- Every artist got lost.

- As a creative, you have to "go there" even if you have no idea how you're going to get out.

- You are creative. Believe it. Own it. Use it.

- *In the beginning, God created.* Will we pay it forward?

85

Wasted free time is incredibly expensive. Where do I waste the most time?

Time is the most valuable commodity you have, especially in your twenties.

Having three kids now, I definitely understand more than ever the importance of being a steward of the time I have. This doesn't mean I'm a machine, constantly being productive every second of the day. But it does mean, if I have two hours to get something done, I better do it!

Wasted free time is incredibly expensive.

Do you have a propensity for turning that five minutes on social media into an hour? Do you have a list of ten must-watch shows? How are you spending your time? Well, it's time to take a time audit of your day.

In an average day, how much time do you waste on stuff that doesn't add anything to your life or move you forward? Be honest. Now multiply the time you waste per day by 7 to get how much time you waste in a week.

If you don't feel like you have enough time to pursue your dreams, maybe this is why.

Dreams are not destroyed by a lack of resources or opportunities; they are silently assassinated by distraction and a lack of focus.

This week, try cutting out one thing that is a big time waster for you. Now you've just been given the gift of time.

86

What is my next right move?

In an interview, Oprah was asked to give her best piece of advice for young people looking to succeed. And of course I love that her advice came in the form of a question—a simple one, yet a life-changing one if we infuse it in our lives.

Ask yourself—"What is the next right move?"

I've realized in my life that I like to dream way more than I like to do. Talking about big ideas, thinking about the what ifs and the possibilities of this big dream happening is like eating caramel popcorn for me—once I've started, it's hard for me to stop.

Yet, just like partaking in my seventh handful of caramel goodness, the big dream that was so tantalizing minutes before starts to have some nauseating effects. The enormity of the dream that excited me minutes before switches to a heavy weight of, "Wait, how in the world am I going to pull this off?"

This is why I really like Oprah's question and advice—"what is the next right move? And then from that space, make the next right move and the next right move and not to be overwhelmed by it because you know your life is bigger than that one moment."

Am I being mentored? Am I being a mentor?

I believe mentor relationships might be the most meaningful relationships you can groom in your twenties, and your whole life.

And I believe we should be mentored and we should be mentoring. When you're mentored, you learn a ton. When you mentor someone else, you might actually learn even more.

Now maybe you're thinking—who am I to mentor anyone? I can't even get my laundry done before it's that heaping pile that takes six loads to finish and I'm wearing swimsuit bottoms for underwear.

I hear you.

But you always have something to offer. You don't have to have all the answers to help someone else with their questions. You can still be there for someone, even when wearing swimsuit underwear.

And when you help someone else find clarity, you typically find a bunch for yourself in return.

Mentoring doesn't always have to look "all kinds of official" either.

Mentoring doesn't always have to look like sitting down together for a formal mentoring session. It can be more every day. For example, being mentored or mentoring in the office might come through many small conversations with someone throughout the day, rather than just one official sit-down meeting every other week.

Not mentoring or being mentored? Below write three possibilities of someone you could mentor and someone who could mentor you. Then reach out to number one on each list.

Mentoring relationships don't have to be a huge time commitment and all kinds of intense. At the heart, mentoring is about sharing wisdom and life experiences with another.

Not sure what you'd talk about? Heck, bring this book with you and walk through the questions. Done and done and done.

THREE PEOPLE I'D LIKE TO MENTOR

1.

2.

3.

THREE PEOPLE I'D LIKE TO BE MENTORED BY

1.

2.

3.

How do I reach out to someone I'd like to meet?

Alright, so we've talked a lot about "relationshipping," now how do we tangibly put that in an email to someone we'd like to meet?

For example, alumni from the high school, college, or graduate school you graduated from are some of the best relationship opportunities you can have.

Jump on your school's alumni database, go to your school's career office, and/or search for alumni in your area on LinkedIn. Even read your college alumni magazine for amazing networking possibilities. Then reach out with a short, creative, three-point email. Literally do a 1. 2. 3.

People read lists, not life stories. Here's how you craft the email.

1) Compliment them on something.

Again, lead with their name and a meaningful compliment. Find their Twitter or LinkedIn profile, website, company, anything, and compliment them on it. Not cheesy, gushy, or fake. Just a few lines of praise that's specific. It shows you've done your homework and instantly draws them into liking you.

2) Say your name, degree (if relevant, and a quick inside joke or comment about your alma mater), and then one line about what you're passionate about, your "why," which aligns with something they're interested in as well.

3) Ask them this simple question: how did you become successful in [enter applicable career field here]?

Then leave the email at that and walk away. Don't even make an ask for a phone call, informational interview, or any further advice.

Same thing applies for more reach *influencers* that you find on LinkedIn and Twitter.

Make a list of 25–50 key influencers in the field or company you'd like to work for, and follow them on Twitter and LinkedIn, if you can. Don't just pick the Mark Cubans and the Jimmy Fallons of the world. Pick some mid-range people who have some pull, but are still accessible.

Then, do you want a fail-proof strategy on how to get them to read your tweets?

You guessed it—compliment them. Give them Twitter-Love. ReTweet. Share articles they've written with a short line of commentary (of course agreeing with theirs). Don't go overboard and Tweet-Stalk, but consistently become an advocate they'll remember.

Maybe they'll follow you back, or even better, they'll check out that legit website you created and see that you're the real, genuine deal, perfect for an opening they've been itching to fill.

SOMEONE
OUT THERE
RIGHT NOW
NEEDS
YOUR DREAM,

AND
NEITHER
OF YOU
KNOW IT.

PAUL ANGONE | *101 QUESTIONS YOU NEED TO ASK IN YOUR TWENTIES* | #101Q

89

The person I reached out to emailed me back; now what should I do?

If the person you're reaching out to responds to your email (which I think you'll find a 75–85% success rate because you're complimenting them and giving them an opportunity to brag about themselves), then ask if you could talk for ten minutes on the phone about the field they work in and learn more about their story and how they became successful.

Key points here. I think at first you should try for a phone call, not a lunch. There is a war for people's time these days. Don't ask for dinner and a movie, and scare them away.

And if you snag a phone call, make sure the conversation is mainly about hearing *their story of success, not yours*. People love talking about themselves and how they ascended from the bottom "coffee fetcher" to the "successfully fine self" they are today.

Then make sure at ten minutes into the call you say, "It's been ten minutes, and I want to be respectful of your time." If the phone call has gone well (especially if you have them talking about themselves), most likely they'll want to talk longer. Or even better, maybe they'll say, "Hey, why don't you swing by the office someday and I can show you around?"

Music to thy ears.

After the call make sure to thank them through email, and give them a Twitter or LinkedIn shout-out if they have an account.

"Just spoke with @_____. Wise, witty, and gracious. Please follow her for superb advice about _____."

Thanking them on Twitter is a nice, public shout-out and creates a brand of gratitude on your end.

Even if you're more introverted, "relationshipping" is for you because it makes meeting new people about them. Don't hide away. Give people meaningful compliments and watch the meaningful connections start to take place.

90

Does my career path create the life I want? Well, if the thought of doing your boss's job 15 years from now makes you throw up a little in your mouth, that's not a good sign.

Do you love your job, but it's pretty much a given that you're working 70 hour weeks? And your boss works 80 hours. Or maybe your career is filled with purpose and passion, yet it doesn't really pay the bills? It's a strange paradox when you love your job, but you don't love the lifestyle it creates.

Does studying, researching, and becoming more proficient in your career give you energy or drain it?

Does learning about your industry or craft give you life or take from it?

If becoming a master of your craft is something you're avoiding, it's either time to fully dive in or it's time to pick a new craft.

This might mean you have to make a difficult decision about the kind of life you want to live. But I promise it will be easier to make that choice now, than when a house, spouse, and a few kids are in the picture. Choose a healthy life, not just a successful career.

91

Am I being stereotyped in my office for being a twentysomething? If so, what do I do about it?

The stereotypes and generalizations are still running rampant about twentysomethings today, a list of new articles coming out every day that definitively tell all of us, without a doubt, who Millennials or Gen Z are. As I wrote in *101 Secrets For Your Twenties*, "Generational stereotyping is all the rage these days. For some reason we think a generation can be summed up with a two-paragraph label like a box of Wheat Thins."

The same old buzzwords are being thrown around about everything twentysomethings "are doing wrong." We dare not stereotype based on gender, religion, race, or sexual orientation, but if you stereotype based on age you've got a front-cover story.

And if you're twentysomething, your managers might have their own stereotypes about you based on your age before you even tackle a project, especially as a "Millennial."

The stereotypes might be subtle or incredibly pronounced, but you must be aware of how you are being perceived. Then do your best to take those stereotypes to the shredder and into the outgoing trash.

If you feel like you're being stereotyped because of your age, your best ally is quiet confidence—a humble consistency that shows up and gets the job done. You don't argue with them about your skill set, you just show them every single day how awesome your skills are.

It's a tough, thankless gig, but soon, very soon, you'll prove to them that you're a person, not an age range.

Try not to be too frustrated about being labeled an entitled, narcissistic Millennial. Instead, focus on being an UnMillennial, proving that you are everything they think you are not.

92

What are my Top 3 nonnegotiables in life and work?

I think it's crucial for all of us to begin to define what is a nonnegotiable for us in life and what is something that we're willing to sacrifice.

This idea definitely ties into your soul values and story in the Signature Sauce questions, so please feel free to reference those questions as you answer this one.

What are your nonnegotiables?

For example, after working for a few years in cubicle jobs, I started learning that a nonnegotiable for me was being able to work on creating my own thing that I feel has deeper meaning. Whether I was pursuing my own creative efforts on the side for years or going full-time on the side hustle, I started understanding that to feel like my life and work have significance, I need to be hammering away at projects of my own creation that are tied into meeting a bigger need.

Write a list of your Top 3 nonnegotiables as you can best articulate them right now.

1.

2.

3.

93

Have I not been able to find my dream job yet because I haven't created it?

The gatekeepers are gone.

What I mean by that is . . . the concept that there is one way of doing things, where there is only one path to go down, where you have to convince one type of person to let you through to achieve your dream, is a thing of the past.

Sure, there are still key influences and leaders in different career fields that can help or hurt your progress in achieving your dream. However, with the increasing number of tools and technologies at our disposal, we have the ability to find a different way, to be fluid and flexible in creating a different path to go down to achieve success.

For example, websites like Upwork are where you can either be a freelancer or hire a freelancer, and work with people from all over the world doing graphic design, branding, copywriting, computer programming, website design, etc. I've used resources like this to help code my website AllGroanUp.com, something I couldn't have afforded by going to a big company where I would have been just a small fish.

There's this army of freelancers and creatives out there—this fluid and flexible group, working at coffee shops and coworking offices, trading services with each other for the other person's expertise.

There's not one standard way to have a career these days. And maybe your "career" will encompass many different jobs that somehow all work together.

When I describe to people what I do, working on my own as an author, speaker, consultant, etc., I describe my life like a wheel where I'm constantly putting in and removing different spokes to keep the whole thing turning. My career is many different things fitting within one thing.

So maybe finding the right job for you has been difficult because that job doesn't technically exist yet. Whether you're currently working in a company or striking out on your own, what does fulfilled, successful work look like to you? Can you shift your current role in your company to incorporate more of those aspects? Can you begin working on the side to create your own job that fits more of your ideas for "career" success?

What does your wheel look like that keeps your career turning in a positive direction? You don't need to wait for, nor should you expect, your dream job to magically fall in your lap. Maybe instead your dream job is hidden right now, waiting for you to uncover and create it.

94

Success in your 20s and 30s is about consistency, humility, and many other unsexy words that won't make the Twentysomething Hallmark Collection. Have I developed a long view to make success a possibility?

Our generation gets knocked for having big, unrealistic dreams.

Yet, I love our "unrealistic" dreams. You can't stay realistic and create something new.

If you're going to create something new, by definition it's not going to be real until you make it so.

However, if you don't develop a long view, then your dream will die before it has a chance to be born. Developing a long view is a skill. It's the ability to see beyond the immediate setbacks, failures, and successes.

You can't let your dream always be do-or-die depending on the ebb and flow of the day.

Your twenties are an Ironman marathon, not a sprint. When you develop a long-view, you're able to take the gritty steps toward your future, even when the present feels enveloped with sullen winter-gray.

When you develop a long view of your dreams, failure becomes a slight detour, not a complete rockslide blocking your path.

95

Sometimes I feel hopeless. How do I fight for hope?

As I wrote in *101 Secrets For Your Twenties:*

"The most underrated tool you have to rocking your 20s is hope. Sometimes you have to climb hills and declare the truth of your bright future instead of the reality of your lackluster present. Sometimes you have to war for hope."

And we need to help each other fight for hope. War for hope together so you don't fight this war alone.

Yet, where does hope come from? I wasn't the first to ask this question, that's for sure. Psalm 121 kind of covered this before I did in one of the most reassuring and hopeful chapters of the Bible. The psalmist's source of hope when life feels daunting and overwhelming? "My help comes from the LORD, who made heaven and earth."

There's permanence, a rootedness to that hope. I look at the mountains in front of me, and instead of seeing insurmountable obstacles, I see the God who made them. I see the God of heaven and earth saying, "*Relax.* I've got this."

Whether God feels close to you and present in your life or as distant as your crazy uncle Joe you haven't spoken to in fifteen years, give this hope a chance.

This hope is your "even so."

I feel this pain, I feel this loss, it is real, it hurts.

Yet, **even so**, I believe in the hope of my future.

Even so, I believe this pain isn't permanent.

Even so, I believe this season will change. I believe God's got this and got me.

Even so, I hope.

It's not a naïve hope oblivious to the pain. It's a permanent refuge as the pain swirls all around. If hope is not rooted, it will be swept away in the raging winds.

96

Should I be asking myself, "What will I do in five years?" Or should I be asking, "In five years, who do I want to be?"

So what do you see yourself doing in 5–10 years?

It's the go-to college graduation party/job interview question that's supposed to be enlightening, yet usually leaves you feeling like you just tried to eat the whole graduation cake all by yourself.

What will I be doing in five years? Gosh, hand me that crystal ball, Confucius, and I will spin you a tale.

Instead of asking what will you do in five years, ask yourself—**who do I want to *be* in five years?**

What you will do is going to shift, change, pivot, and adjust. If your whole vision for the future is based on some concrete definition of what you will be doing, when what you're doing doesn't turn out like your five-year plan said it should, you will feel like your face is constantly slamming into that same concrete.

What kind of person are you becoming? Instead of chasing every new puddle and stream, what well are you going to draw from?

In 5–10 years you will do some amazing things, I truly believe that. But I promise you'll do more amazing things if you're focused on who you are becoming more than just what you're doing along the way.

So when the next person asks you what you will be doing in five years, tell them who you hope to become. Tell them about the *doing* that will burst forth from your *being*.

97

What do I need to do while I wait to do what I was born to do?

Kurt Warner was an NFL football quarterback, Super Bowl winner, most valuable player, and now a Hall of Fame inductee, the highest award a football player can receive.

Yet, if you know Kurt's story you know of his NFL dream coming to an end before it really started. Of being cut by the only team that took a chance on him. Of taking care of his kids during the day while his wife worked, and then stocking shelves at a grocery store through the night. He'd hit rock bottom and wasn't sure if there was going to be a way up.

However, Kurt kept the hope. He warred for it. He didn't just stay there in those grocery aisles expecting his circumstance to magically change. No, he tried out for the Arena Football League, a lesser-known style of football that didn't pay much and didn't have a bright light at the end of the tunnel. But at least there was a glimmer of hope. Playing in the Arena Football league wasn't his dream, but it sure was a heck of a lot closer than throwing cereal boxes around at 2:00 a.m.

And through one not-so-chance encounter after another, Kurt would have people take a chance on him, like the coach for the St. Louis Rams, Dick Vermeil, who would out-vote some of his other coaches to keep Kurt on the team because he saw something special in Kurt and wanted to see if what he saw was real.

The rest is history. Kurt would break records. Win countless awards. Win the Super Bowl. Win the respect of teammates and fans. And in his Hall of Fame speech he'd say:

"Sometimes you gotta do what you gotta do while you're waiting to do what you were born to do. . . . But . . . there's a point of no return, and I was backing myself into that corner. If I wanted different results, I needed to change my course."

Do what you need to do, yet don't stop making baby steps, if need be, toward what you were born to do. If it can work for a grocery store clerk turned Hall of Fame quarterback, it can work for you.

98

ADULT

What's the worst that can happen?

Having your worst fears realized can be the best thing to happen to you. Because you quickly realize that the worst outcome you could possibly imagine isn't actually as bad as you thought.

Take for example, when I was trying to get my first book published for years. The worst thing I could've imagined was every publisher saying no. Well, after numerous "we like the book, but . . ." it became fairly clear that my worst fear was curling up in my lap and not going anywhere.

Yet, if my "worst fear" wouldn't have happened, I would not have started my website AllGroanUp.com. I would have not gone back to school to get my master's degree. I would not have struggled to become a better writer and grown in character, perseverance, and humility. I would not have been forced to build a stronger foundation, find another way, and be able to help others do the same.

Basically, a publisher saying yes to me as an insecure twenty-three-year-old would've been the worst thing to happen to me, not the other way around.

As Conan O'Brien aptly put it in a college graduation speech at Dartmouth University after his fallout and failures of having the *Tonight Show* taken away from him: "There are few things more liberating in this life than having your worst fear realized. . . . It is our failure to become our perceived ideal that ultimately defines us and makes us unique. . . . Your perceived failure can become a catalyst for profound reinvention. . . . Disappointment will come. The beauty is that through disappointment you can gain clarity, and with clarity comes conviction and true originality."

So as you take steps toward your dream—ask yourself, "What's the worst that can happen?"

Usually our worst fears are not nearly as terrifying as we make them. Once they happen, we actually realize they were the exact catalyst we needed to make a change and start something new.

So if you're sitting in front of an email you're scared to send, a project you're nervous to start, a relationship you're thinking of pursuing—what's the worst that can happen? It not working out? Well, it's for sure not going to happen if you don't try.

The actual worst thing that can happen is you not giving it a shot at all. That would be the worst. Not a failed outcome. The worst is floating aimlessly in the black abyss of never trying and never knowing. That's the scariest place to exist.

When the box you've placed yourself in shatters, after the initial trauma wears off, you realize there was a whole other world out there. Waiting for you to step into. You just needed something to smash it open. And usher you in.

99

(ADULT)

What's the best that can happen?

Yet, on the other hand, think about *the best* that can happen if you try. How many people could your dream help? How much more meaningful will your life feel? How important will this success be for your family?

I think a lot about the long-term effects and how the progress I make now will have an exponential effect on my children later.

On that note, hey kids, if you're reading this book in your twenties, first, thanks for reading a book filled with advice from me since you've had to live with my advice for your whole life! Second, I know you're going to start your race much further down the path than I did. I keep striving to push my ceiling even higher so that you can make that your floor. Use it. Leverage it. I can't wait to see how high the ceiling becomes for *your* kids!

Think about the best that can happen. And chances are, what you're able to imagine as the best now, will not even be nearly as amazing as it's going to become later!

If I could write my kids advice now that they will read in their 20s, what would I tell them?

Since I just wrote my kids a little note, I think it's only fitting that I give you the chance to do the same. What do you want to tell your kids (or future kids) when they are sitting where you sit? What truths are percolating inside of you that you want them to taste? How cool would it be to give them this book decades from now so that they can see firsthand your process, your struggle, and your truths.

101

If not now, when?

There will always be a great reason why you shouldn't begin pursuing your dream.

There will always be reasons why you shouldn't move forward, or why you shouldn't strive for more.

There will always be wonderful distractions. There will always be very real obstacles. There will always be vocal "Reality Checkers." There will be reasons why today is not the day.

But if not now, when?

If not you, then who?

Don't wait for the perfect plan. Don't wait for the perfect opportunity. Don't wait for inspired inspiration.

The world needs your Signature Sauce. We need the flavor only you can bring. It's time to live life like you mean it because the world needs the story you bring.

There's this fun little trend going on to bash the uniqueness out of you. Some will treat you like you should be put under fluorescent lights, in a tiny cubicle, on an assembly line, putting together fluorescent lights for tiny cubicles.

Sure, some of us haven't always applied our uniqueness in very humble or unique ways.

Yet, optimism is not a character flaw. Hope is not naïve. Every dream is impossible until it's not.

Create. Make. Dream. Do.

Create. Make. Dream. Do.

If not now, when?

If not you, then who?

Removable lists
of all 101 Questions
by category

ADULTING TO WIN

1. What's the best way to break up with myself?
2. Am I struggling to make it appear like I'm not struggling?
5. Are there dark days ahead?
7. Am I seeing the other side of people's Instagram photos (you know, the side they're not exactly posting pictures of)?
10. Should I really post this?
14. How do I make a choice when I don't know what to choose?
15. What is fear keeping me from doing? Is it worth it?
25. Instead of trying to solve life's big problems late at night as an anxious exhaustion swallows me like a black fog, should I try something more productive, like, you know, going to sleep?
29. Can I laugh at myself?
32. Am I being brave enough to be awkward?
35. How do I combat my anxiety?
36. What is my anxiety telling me?
40. Should I be asking—"Is life fair?"
46. How do I stop "infotainment" from slapping me in the face every five seconds and taking my lunch money?
50. Am I bathing in disappointment like a cat taking a nap in its own litter box?
52. How do I grab my fear by the ears and snarl at it?
60. What am I going to regret NOT doing?
62. How do I find my "77% sure" and just move forward?
77. Am I building my Grown-Up Sandcastle too close to the ocean?
79. Am I holding my dreams hostage and demanding that I pay the ransom?
81. If I do this now, how am I going to feel about this later?
85. Wasted free time is incredibly expensive. Where do I waste the most time?
94. Have I developed a long view to make success a possibility?
96. Should I be asking myself, "What will I do in five years?" Or should I be asking, "In five years, who do I want to be?"
98. What's the worst that can happen?
99. What's the best that can happen?
100. If I could write my kids advice now that they will read in their 20s, what would I tell them?
101. If not now, when?

4. If I'm going to pursue a big dream, am I willing to drive a 1993 Honda Civic Hatchback with no power steering, no air conditioning, and no right mirror for 15 years?

17. What is my "Significant Why"?

26. How do I keep doing inspiring work even when I feel completely uninspired?

28. On a scale of 1–10, how would I rank my online social networking?

31. Do you work hard and are you easy to work with?

33. How do I stop networking and start "relationshipping"?

34. How do I do relationshipping better?

41. Where's the future of work headed, and what does having a successful career look like?

43. How do I keep my wick from being doused with gasoline and burned at both ends?

47. Do your actions back up your ambitions? Does your behavior back up your words?

48. Comfort and challenge don't play nice together at the same table. Am I looking for a challenging job or a comfortable one?

49. It's a lot easier to do something successful once than it is to sustain it. So the question is—*why are one-hit wonders, one-hit wonders?*

59. Am I putting myself in places where I can meet people and start "relationshipping" more?

80. During an average day at work, what's my Dread/Tolerate/Love percentage breakdown?

84. Creating something new is a courageous fight against "the way it's always been." What will I create?

86. What is my next right move?

88. How do I reach out to someone I'd like to meet?

89. The person I reached out to emailed me back; now what should I do?

90. Does my career path create the life I want?

91. Am I being stereotyped in my office for being a twentysomething? If so, what do I do about it?

92. What are my Top 3 nonnegotiables in life and work?

93. Have I not been able to find my dream job yet because I haven't created it?

96. Should I be asking myself, "What will I do in five years?" Or should I be asking, "In five years, who do I want to be?"

97. What do I need to do while I wait to do what I was born to do?

101. If not now, when?

RELATIONSHIPPING

2. Am I struggling to make it appear like I'm not struggling?

3. What kind of friendships do I have—Jetpack Friends, helping me fly, or Anvil-Friends, repeatedly pulling me down into some dark basement?

6. Do I love from my insecurities or from my strengths?

11. Everything you think you know about marriage flies out the window once you're actually married. So what's the best way to know if you're actually ready to get married?

12. One of the best ways to forget your problems is by helping someone else with theirs, and one of the best ways to find perspective is by looking outside yourself. So ask yourself—*who can I help today?* There's no lack of "Help Wanted" signs.

13. Have I told anyone where I'm going?

27. Am I trying to kill a rat in my life by taking the rat poison myself?

28. On a scale of 1–10, how would I rank my online social networking?

30. Why do some people have great marriages while others have complete wrecks before they even make it to the highway?

33. How do I stop networking and start "relationshipping"?

34. How do I do relationshipping better?

37. Do I want to become mashed together for life with the person I'm dating (or hoping to date)?

38. Do I see that finding someone attractive is much more profound and complex than just thinking they're smoking hot?

39. What is love?

44. Do I have anyone on my "Dream Team?"

45. Do I have any glaring Critics, Cynics, or "Reality Checkers" in my life that are doing their best to hold me back?

58. Am I recognizing the "not-so-chance" encounters in my life?

59. Am I putting myself in places where I can meet people and start "relationshipping" more?

66. Do my soul values repel or compel my significant other's soul values?

67. Do I like who I am when I'm with my partner?

68. Does my partner challenge me to be a better, authentic version of myself?

69. Are my partner and I communicating about the crazy ways we've learned how to communicate crazily?

70. Have I tackled my relationship monsters?

71. In our marriage or dating relationship, have we discussed our vision for the future together? What does the story of our marriage look like? (If I'm not dating anyone, but want to, what do I envision a fulfilling, healthy marriage to look like?)

72. If I'm being brutally honest with myself and this dating relationship, do I absolutely trust my partner with my life?

76. What kind of parent do I want to be?

87. Am I being mentored? Am I being a mentor?

88. How do I reach out to someone I'd like to meet?

89. The person I reached out to emailed me back; now what should I do?

101. If not now, when?